The Death Company

THE
DEATH
COMPANY

CRISTOFORO BASEGGIO

Translated by
Gabriele Costarella

ANTELOPE HILL PUBLISHING

Second printing 2022.

Originally published in Italian as *La Compagnia Della Morte* by Istituto Editoriale Veneto, 1929.

Translated into English 2021 by Gabriele Costarella, Taccuino@protonmail.com

Cover art by Swifty.
Edited by Jill McKraken.
Formatted by Margaret Bauer.

Antelope Hill Publishing
www.antelopehillpublishing.com

Paperback ISBN-13: 978-1-956887-42-6
EPUB ISBN-13: 978-1-953730-71-8

"The world is an ancient palace that overhangs from above.
Walking straight ahead you will hit your head on its beam, so
you will bend before the beam that is about to hit you.

I would rather break my forehead than bend my back."

SANDOR PETÖFI (1823–1849)
Hungarian poet and liberal revolutionary

Contents

Translator's Foreword ix

Commendations of Major Baseggio xii

Introduction...xiii

Preface by Giovanni Borelli xvi

Preface by Cristoforo Baseggio xxiii

Acclaim and Reviews.. xxv

The Death Company

Main Narrative 3

The Conquest of Mount Salubio 11

The Taking of Colle San Giovanni (The Maso Valley) 18

Reconnaissance on Ranch Palauro.. 22

The Volunteer Explorer Company Arditi Baseggio 27

The Roncegno Raid... 33

Night Raid on Torcegno and Roncegno 36

The Glockenthurm Raid 42

Attack on Montalon 47

Occupation of Marter 52

The Emergency Expedition to Forcella Magna......................... 55

The Attack and Conquest of Mount Collo 57

The Conquest of the Great Volto Trench............................... 62

The Conquest of Mount Saint Osvaldo.................................. 69

Conclusion..78

Appendix A: Correspondence from Military Personnel 81

Appendix B: Newspaper Articles 94

Appendix C: Letter by Mario Dei Gaslini 117

Appendix D: Poem by G. Vacchetta to the Death Company........120

Translator's Foreword

There is no clearer demonstration of indomitable will than in the works of Cristoforo Baseggio, the author of *The Death Company*. At the commission of Antelope Hill Publishing, I have carefully extrapolated and translated his work. I say carefully, for the spirit of this book is a delicate being. It flows from line to line, with every episode narrated by Baseggio showing unwavering loyalty, comradery, and courage. Yet, it also carries a heartbreaking and terrible martial sense. This consciousness is woven into the epic scope of the Death Company.[1] Understate the significance of their sacrifice, and it will have been in vain.

The Death Company is more than an excellent military memoir. It is Major Cristoforo Baseggio's war cry to the halls of the heroes, anxious to take his place among them. It was he who led the first *Arditi*[2] Company, those prestigious special forces that defined the Italian heroic narrative of war. By war's end, Arditi companies had swelled to 18,000 strong. Among this mass of honorable fighters, Baseggio claims a unique place for himself and his men. English readers will note that much of his work seems rather self-aggrandizing for an autobiography; Italian lacks the severe Anglophone taboo against self-praise. This work is not only a historical account, but also openly makes the case that events

---

[1] The Death Company was the nickname of Cristoforo Baseggio's company. Other names used included: Arditi Company Cristoforo Baseggio, Ardite Explorers Baseggio, Explorers Company Arditi Baseggio, Arditi Company Baseggio, Arditi Explorers, Volunteer Reconnaissance Company Arditi Baseggio, Voluntary Arditi Company Baseggio, Volunteer Explorer Company Arditi Baseggio, Explorers Company, Baseggio Company, Explorers Arditi Company, Arditi Company, Volunteer Company Baseggio, Baseggio Explorers, Arditi Baseggio Company, and Arditi Volunteer Company.

[2] [The name given to the Italian assault troops/divisions. It also derives some meaning from the French word *hardi* (strong, brutish, hard). Refer to the note on *arditismo*.]

happened a certain way because of certain men, more in the vein of Caesar's *Gallic Wars* than a modern, matter-of-fact account of events.

Let us examine the dire situation that befell Major Baseggio (at that time a Colonel) and the entire eastern Italian front during the First World War.

The Austrians had taken control of key mountain locations along the eastern Italian front. The Fassa Alps were well guarded and would take many men's lives if assaulted. Mount Collo and Mount Saint Osvaldo were excellent strategic positions for an all-out offensive that was already in the works behind the grim vista of the *Glockenthurm*.[3] Men watched from their trenches, hiding along parapets with their guns pointing into no-man's-land. Tension in the Italian lines had taken the form of a grim silence, as if the men already knew their doom was approaching and wished nothing more than for it to envelop them quickly. The Italian High Command was paralyzed, using outdated methodology and wasting time in failed assaults and flanking maneuvers that would end with many bloody and dead men.

In a command post not too far away from the incumbent action, sat an officer. A veteran of many mountain engagements in Africa, he was a man of strict discipline, for whom every dead man under his command was a painful stab to the heart. He watched unfolding events before him and saw not incoming defeat, but a new ray of hope.

That ray radiated forth, not from the sun, but from the black shirts and golden insignia of men who formed his company in the coming months. Colonel Baseggio asked his superiors if they would allow him to create a new company, not based on doctrinal tactics, but on new, intrepid actions which he called "*ardite*."[4] The generals accepted this request and deployed their resources to create an infantry company which influenced not only the outcome of the war and other armies of Europe at that time, but also future armies across the globe. That company was called the Arditi Company Cristoforo Baseggio, also known as the Death Company.

---

[3] [Literally "Bell Tower." A mountain town that was turned into a fortress by the Austro-Hungarian military.]

[4] [Ardite is used to describe actions done in typical ardito (singular of arditi) fashion, as in defiant actions carried out with little regard for one's personal safety or the size and extent of an enemy's opposing forces. These were actions which sought an outcome of honor and glory. Refer to the note on *arditismo*.]

Men flocked from all parts of the Royal Army to join the Death Company: military police, special forces, and troops from all divisions volunteered to join Baseggio's new quest to vanquish their nation's enemy. Some were even criminals. Regardless of their backgrounds, they all came with purpose, reinvigorated by their commander, their illusions cast aside by a new faith. It was a faith in nation and in combat, which demanded honor above all else.

These men would go on to conquer entire defensive positions that larger armies could not. They were known by name even to their Austrian adversaries. The whole world watched as these first *sturmtruppen*[5] made their way, not solely out of military academies, but out of the mud and snow of the Carso Mountains. They were neither nobles nor knights, yet they created a legion equal to the Order of Malta in military achievements.

Note: Quite often in his memoir, Baseggio refers to "graduates" and "graduated soldiers," soldiers in the Italian Army who held a "diploma of war" from an academic military school, though neither designation necessarily denotes commissioned officers or sergeants. There is no direct equivalent in the English-speaking military tradition. Perhaps the closest modern equivalent would be soldiers in modern American armed forces who are granted the title of "Ranger," having passed through Ranger School of Light Infantry Leadership. To denote the status of Baseggio's "graduates" as normal soldiers who were granted additional status and responsibility, this translation refers to them as "ensigns." This term is for the extremely junior officers of the Napoleonic British Army. They were assigned to keep formations in line, act as messengers, and perform other tasks a common soldier was responsible for, but with a greater degree of education, professionalism, and respect than regular troops. This provides the nearest functional military equivalent that an English reader would recognize.

All translations in this text, including the footnotes, are taken from Italian, unless otherwise indicated.

---

[5] [Italian or German for "stormtroopers."]

Commendations of Major Baseggio

- Awarded on May 29th, 1913: Nominated Knight of the Italian Crown for meritorious actions during the Italian-Turkish Theatre (1912–1913)

- Awarded on November 27th, 1915: Meritorious Promotion to the rank of Captain

- Awarded on May 6th, 1916: Medal of Merit for the volunteers of the Austrian-Italian War

- Awarded on July 22th, 1916: Bronze Medal for Military Valor (August 24th, 1915)

- Awarded on August 21st, 1917: Meritorious Promotion to the rank of Major

- Awarded on April 11st, 1918: Silver Medal for Military Valor (August–September 1917)

- Awarded on March 4th, 1919: Cross of War

- Awarded on December 4th, 1919: Commemorative Medal for the Italian-Turkish War

- Awarded on June 5th, 1920: Badge for War Efforts with Two Stars

- Awarded on June 21st, 1920: British Silver Medal (War Office Bulletin, August 1916)

- Awarded on May 19th, 1921: War Remembrance Medal (1915–1918)

- Awarded on February 12th, 1925: Silver Medal for Military Valor (May–June 1915)

- Awarded on February 12th, 1925: Silver Medal for Military Valor (July 3th–6th, 1916)

- Received the French War Cross (August–September 1917)

- Nominated Knight of the Order of the Saintly Maurizio and Lazzaro for meritorious actions in the theatre of war

Introduction

Twelve years after I disbanded the Death Company, I can, without being accused of vanity, carry out my duty towards both the dead and survivors by recounting the acts of faith and martial feats that are now enshrined in history. They will forever live in the memories of our descendants. The Death Company left on the mount most of its brave men, consecrated by glory and red tracks of courageous blood.

This re-evocation will tell the Italian people, especially our young, that spirit governs the material. A few zealous souls can inspire the masses by their example, awakening their sentiments towards valor and overwhelming an enemy, even if they are more numerous or better equipped.

This return to historical truth and facts about the war, which have been ignored by many, but are engraved into legend, will serve to correct some deficiencies that jealousy and over-competitiveness try in vain to insinuate into reality and historical fact.

These pages simply deal with facts and historical episodes. Without any literary claim, they tell of mighty deeds, of valiant men who knew how to dare the impossible. They speak of concerns, hardships, fierce brawls, and victories that accompanied the conquests of *Colle*[6] San Giovanni, of Montalon, of Marter, of Mount Collo, of the Great Volto Trench, of Mount Saint Osvaldo. They say that it is possible for Italians to love their country with sacrifice and death. They say that it is possible to be covetous of one's rights and obedient to one's duties, when it is profoundly and spontaneously felt and not imposed, and when faith, *l'ardire*,[7] the love of country and of family are vestiges of blood and of elect noble souls. Ultimately, over time, citizens give to their country

---

[6] [Short form of *collina*, meaning "hill."]
[7] [Courage, bravery or daring.]

liberty, greatness, and independence.

The facts herein recorded have no greater value, in and of themselves, than many other facts of war and would not need to be highlighted, if it were not for the fact that they consecrate an idea. They express an act of faith and are further proof that *arditismo,*[8] *the exaltation of personal valor and the spirit of sacrifice,* opposed in war the static tendencies that accompanied a military education and discipline more formal than substantial. Facts are, therefore, of immense moral and historical value. With the disbanding of the first Arditi Company, its few survivors considered it their apostolic mission to disseminate and inspire the spirit of the *ardito*[9] throughout the entire army. Later, assault departments were born, along with major tactical formations of the Arditi.

With the Arditi, I, their guide and commander in war, heir, and beacon of their ardite in peace, later infused this animated spirit into the fighting people of the first grisly battles of our Revolution. We moved to assault the regime in the holy name of country and root out all menacing Bolshevism and unworthy government officials.

I have written these pages, not for vanity or futile love of glory, but as a duty towards my dead, for a sense of justice towards the survivors. They are apostles of a movement of men, who wrote in their blood during both war and peace, unsurmountable pages of history. For those who know that the force behind the command and authority of our government is dignity, strength, and pride in our nation, they will understand the worth of these pages that attempt to give a just tribute of glory to our gallant heroes, and to incite and give an example to all Italians.

Major C. Baseggio

---

[8] [Name given to describe the philosophy and lifestyle of the Arditi. It was best described as a defiant search for danger and adventure, refusing to settle for a tranquil life, placing courage and spiritual fortitude above all else. Arditismo and all words in its semantic region have had their origin mistakenly placed in the Italian verb *ardire* (to burn). The original derivation lies in the French word *hardi* (strong, brutish, hard). It is relevant to note both words share a common origin in *harjdan* (to make hard). The association with *ardire* was made later, due to the Arditi's actions and their people being commonly associated with flames, but it was only a metaphorical correlation. This was due to assonance between the correlated words, not an etymological one.]

[9] [To act in typical ardito fashion, with little care for one's own life, where all is risked for honor and/or victory.]

Bulletin of the Historical Office of the
Major Army Staff Command

The author, in October 1915, instituted an autonomous company of Arditi Explorers, supported by the command of the Fifteenth Division, with the strength of thirteen officers and around four hundred fifty men. In the winter of 1915 and the spring of 1916, it accomplished a series of brilliant operations in the territory assigned to the First Army. The author, who was the valiant department commander, narrates the company's stories in this volume that he presents to the public. In the enclosed volume are numerous documents pertaining to the actions performed by the company, with a preface by Giovanni Borelli[10] at the head. The company was disbanded in April 1916 and could be considered the standard for all successive assault formations, given how much praise they acquired in the last Great War.

N.C.

---

[10] Giovanni Borelli (1867–1932) was an Italian journalist, liberal politician, and soldier. He is best known for having created the PLI or *Partito Liberale Italiano* (Italian Liberals Party). This was the party of Giovanni Giolitti, the Prime Minister before Mussolini.

Preface by Giovanni Borelli

First Edition

I

I give in, hesitantly, to the honorable request of prefacing a few lines for Major Baseggio's book. The reasons for my hesitation are obvious. Certain pages of one's life should be released to the public without introduction, even if the latter have been awarded or invested of authority that I do not possess. If those pages are of a heroic life in the rare and proper sense, if it is desired or wished to assign them to a presenter, then he should at least think of himself as belonging to the same family of heroes by right of conquest or universal acknowledgement.

Then, however, I had to answer to an entirely different order of considerations. I am a contemporary of Cristoforo Baseggio, an *interventista*,[11] side by side with Filippo Corridoni and Benito Mussolini. I consider myself a most humble man, who would have been content to never again lift the veil from off my own name and my own stories. I was close to Gabriele D'Annunzio[12] and Guglielmo Marconi.[13] I marched on Rome with the Italian Fasces of Combat.[14] I found creative

---

[11] [Interventionist. This word specifically refers to those political activists who were in favor of Italy's intervention in the Great War, as opposed to the neutralists, who thought Italy was not ready for a war. Respectively, we find the prominent political influences of the futurists and fascists against the socialists, liberals, and Catholics.]

[12] An aristocratic Italian poet and playwright who served as an army officer in World War I. He was a national war hero and commanded Arditi units in the years after the Death Company was disbanded.

[13] The Italian inventor and electrical engineer who is credited with the invention of the radio and the telegraph system.

[14] This organization was founded by Benito Mussolini and later became the Italian Fascist Party. After the war, it was the official face of the *squadristi* (those who participated in

guidance from the founder of the *Popolo d'Italia*.[15] I was a witness of war from its frontlines, from the essential centers of its consciousness. I participated in the national movement from its origin. I cannot reject the proud request to speak about Major Baseggio. It is an honor and a privilege to be asked to do so.

I have also felt forced to overcome my hesitations with a categorical imperative. For years, I have thought of how a great work should be written to recount our struggle, with all its culminating moments, driving motivations, historically assertable premises, transition phases, the heights reached and the moments of collapse. It should encapsulate both the defeats and victories of our Italian nation. The war, in my estimation, remains the main protagonist. I grasp the essence of it. It inflicted incalculable repercussions on the fabric of the national family, on individuals, on our ideas and customs, on psychology, and on culture and society.

My *Lines for an Italian History of the Arditi and of Arditismo* is dedicated to the willing volunteers of our war and have appeared in the April 1929 issue of *Esercito E Nazione*[16] (Rome, Ministry of War). That fiery chapter outlines the history of war with revelatory passion and could define the Arditi as the origin of all vanguards, the spiritual guarantors of our destiny. It was a heavy commitment to our necessary victory that constituted the incomparable originality of our warrior vocation in the face of overwhelming criticism. It remains forever evident under the successive instrumental transformations and the preliminary scholastic imitators of professionalism. Cristoforo Baseggio is, without a shadow of a doubt, the forefather of these military formations.

I can bear witness to this, in the absence of any personal interest or obligation, although I have never met the man in person. Baseggio understood the need for the Ardito. He understood well the need for men willing to sacrifice everything for victory, not because of some foolish instinct for careless adventure, but because it was imperative to the very outcome of the war and the Italian nation. With his evocative writing of *The Death Company*, Baseggio give us more than a simple

---

squadrismo).

[15] [*The Italian Nation*, an Italian newspaper founded by Benito Mussolini that ran from November 1914 until July 1943.]

[16] [*Army and Nation*, a monthly magazine directed towards Italian officers. It ran from 1927 to 1929, with a decisively Fascist slant.]

retelling of the Arditi's actions. He gives the reader a connection to these men and their achievements, tangible elements of pride and love of comrades and country. It is as if the reader is there amongst the company, marching through the mountain snows and flinging themselves into the trenches with daggers drawn. Those noble pages bring the story of the Arditi to life and bring us closer to not only their victories, but also their sacrifices.

II

We might try to find similarities between the great works of the past, such as those of Machiavelli, and Baseggio's *The Death Company*. His writing flows forth to fashion an altar for those who shed their blood and lost their lives fighting to take Saint Osvaldo. We can draw from Abba's *Noterelle*[17] as an example of a well-written military memoir. In Baseggio's chronicles, we do not find the handsome candor of The Thousand's[18] diarist, but, nonetheless, his account is worthy of praise.

The First Volunteer Company Arditi was formed in October 1915 at the Fifteenth Division Command Center, under Lieutenant General Farisoglio. The company was comprised of four hundred fifty men and thirteen officers and it took part in various military operations until its destruction on April 6th, 1916, on Saint Osvaldo.

The pages written by Baseggio imbibe themselves with a swelling and athletic *quid*, which determines the character and the intimacy of a bitter and disdainful style. That style sears its way through his account like a hot flame but then shines forth like a flash of thunder. It tastes of sun and glacier. It liberates from the magnanimous heart a sublime love for country and glory, with no equals in the world.

Baseggio originally published parts of his book in October 1923, under the title *The Arditi Company Baseggio*. It was later published in its entirety as *The Death Company*, and it makes a profound contribution to the history of war. It is the definitive work for the military genesis of

---

[17] [Referring to the *Noterelle d'uno dei mille*, "Notes from One of the Thousand," a war memoir written by Giuseppe Cesare Abba.]
[18] "The Thousand" were troops lead by Giuseppe Garibaldi during the unification of Italy.

arditismo. The series of engagements against the Austrians are tied directly to the masculine will and arditismo of the commander of that first exemplary *maniple*.[19] Coupled with his strength and indomitable will, the unfriendliness of the elements, the sacrifices and the deaths required to reach victory itself the company was capable of incredible miracles! The remembrance of the days on Mount Collo (March 1916), the Great Volto Trench (April 3th–5th), and Saint Osvaldo (April 6th) will serve as a continual reminder to our posterity of the inherent virtues of Italians. It will remind them of the honest ideal of valor and of national pride.

The Arditi were continually faced with twelve, sixteen, eighteen hours of marching in the unforgiving winter Alps. They faced an enemy entrenched in formidable and expertly constructed fortifications. They faced nature itself and the dangers of the mountains. There were fresh, young soldiers like Lieutenant Galluzzo; soldiers in their fifties like Baseggio; patricians like Count Casati (who would later become a colonel, then a Senator, and then a Minister); doctors and veterinarians like Vacchetta and Signorelli; journalists like Umerini; and professors like Galante. They hailed from all regions, from the north and from the south. They came from every wing of the army: *Alpini*,[20] *Finanzieri*,[21] *Bersaglieri*,[22] and all the other miscellaneous units. Men of questionable lineage, mode of dress, and physical complexion. They had an unescapable, or what was believed to be unescapable, heretical notion of formal discipline. Nevertheless, they were organized into a successful

---

[19] [Latin for a subdivision of the Roman legion consisting of either 60 or 120 men.]

[20] [Rangers who focused on elite mountain operations. The singular form is *Alpino*. The Alpini are the Italian Army's specialist mountain infantry units. Created in 1872, it is the oldest active mountain infantry worldwide.]

[21] [The *Arma dei Finanzieri*, or *Guardia di Finanza*, was an Italian law enforcement agency. Like the *Carabinieri* (Carabineers), it was militarized and served the Ministry of Economy. It primarily protects the financial interests of Italy by combating fraud and smuggling, but it also protects its borders in military-police fashion. An officer of the *Guardia di Finanza* is called a *finanziere* (financier). This can also translate to "Customs Officer" or "Financial Police."]

[22] [Shock troopers and elite light infantry. The Bersaglieri can be easily recognized by the long black capercaillie feathers on their helmets. General Alessandro La Mormora created them as an efficient substitute for cavalry in the army of the Kingdom of Sardinia in 1836. They were specialists in maneuver warfare, but also served as sharpshooters. Benito Mussolini was among their ranks and was wounded during his service in World War I.]

fighting force.

Within Baseggio beat a heart of pure fire, a veritable "mocker of death."[23] It can be inferred through the accounts of his devoted soldiers that he was no ordinary commander. Lieutenant Vacchetta da Bracciano wrote to him on March 28th, 1923:

> After many years, upon returning to our homeland, I had only one wish: seeing you again. Soon I will leave again. My life is that of a gypsy: the desert, the tent, the forest, the sun that chokes me, the sand, the wind that burns my eyes and dries them of every tear, the solitude. There are my dreams, my life, my sickness. My motto is "to stop is to die."

None of the honorable medals bestowed on Cristoforo Baseggio gave him the proper recognition deserved by one who survived Saint Osvaldo.

III

It is necessary for me to go further and to say more. The immortal spirit of our war is enshrined in the sacrifices made by those brave volunteers. They are the next line of protagonists in this book. These half-fascists[24] seemed at most to have been born with the Red Shirt[25] on. Martial and religious voluntarism can be found in all of them. Fascism, under the boot of that wounded volunteer of Predappio,[26] has won, and it will win. It can add to its conquest the safeguard of the territory of the Italian nation and the integral vision in the office of the Pope through its institutional super-nationality.

Cristoforo Baseggio, tragically, for the sake of victory, fought against the Austria of the Hangman,[27] and threw all his company right

---

[23] Referring to the December 18th, 1922, edition of the literary criticism and art magazine *Meridiano di Roma* (Rome's Meridian). It was a notable publication that ran weekly from 1936 to 1943. Among its associates was Julius Evola.

[24] [The original word is *Mussoliniani*.]

[25] Reference to Garibaldi's troops, not Bolshevism.

[26] Referring to Mussolini. Predappio is the town where he was born.

[27] Nickname given to the Austrian King Franz Joseph. Ironically, he is always portrayed as being hanged himself, maybe alluding to the fragility of his state.

into the arms of death. Its martyrdom—willing or unwilling—transcends space and time. Arditismo is a way of life, a voluntary honor and privilege, held forever in the history of our nation. It is the very struggle of men to triumph over evil and preserve a perfect future. Arditismo, as a necessary and formidable connection to the spirit, is both a religious and educational experience. It can be recognized by its specific traits in the workings of a nation as it has worked itself into the fabric of national history.

Regarding Saint Osvaldo, when Cristoforo Baseggio conquered the position, he turned around, and he did not find an officer of the company who was not unharmed or dead. He reorganized the bloody survivors, a small maniple of fifty-four, and lined them up under enemy fire. He examined their weapons and realized there was not a single round of ammunition left. He put himself at the head of the maniple and ordered, "Count as two!" Then he proceeded to march them, in parade formation, before the Austrian machine guns as if they were in *Piazza d'Armi*.[28] It was indeed a display of the highest expression of prowess and control of the self. The Austrians were so astonished that they stopped firing and watched the remaining Arditi march down the mountain.

Major Cristoforo Baseggio is more than just a warrior. He is an apostle of arditismo. In *Lines for an Italian History of the Arditi and of Arditismo*, I wrote:

Arditismo is made up by the fundamental characteristics of unshakable will and discipline. It is law that pushes against instincts. Its followers are accustomed to action at any hour. They are old friends with sleeplessness and endless marching. Arditismo becomes a category of the Spirit, a militia above all militias, and enacts in its social bonds the principles of youth against corrupting forces. It opposes the often-artificial madness of negation for negation's sake, and especially opposes academic sophistry. It has dealt with the parliamentary illusion of

---

[28] [Weapons Square. It was a plaza in Turin built by the house of Savoy. It was designed to hold the Royal Army's large displays and parades.]

impotence, and the negation of all genuine hierarchical positions and their relative possibilities.

Considering this panoramic description of arditismo, the evocative pages of Cristoforo Baseggio's book take hold of the ideal with an iron fist. I dearly hope that his work will be widely distributed among the army. We cannot return to the attitudes and ideologies of 1915. With that in mind, it is not surprising that there would be criticism and disapproval of Baseggio's work, much of it from within the upper ranks of the Italian Army. Indeed, most of the critics were originally opposed to the creation of the Arditi Company. In hindsight, they cannot argue, with much voracity, that the creation of the company was a detriment to the army and the entire war effort. Indeed, its creation was the exact opposite. It was the division leader General Farisoglio who welcomed the proposal made by Captain Baseggio. He also had approval from the commander of the First Army, Roberto Brusati, and from General Andrea Graziani, head of His Majesty's Army. They understood the value of Baseggio's vision, especially General Graziani. He stood by Baseggio without any reservations. There were other early supporters, like General Clerici, Colonel Spiller and Lieutenant General Sailer, who belonged to the Major Army Staff.

Major Cristoforo Baseggio has given of himself wholeheartedly in writing *The Death Company*. He has done a great service to the men of his company, all the fallen heroes of that glorious vanguard. Mother Mary, protect Cristoforo Baseggio and all the survivors of the Death Company. The debt Italy owes to them will not soon be repaid.

Giovanni Borelli
Fontevivo (from the *Rifugio Margherita*[29])
Parma, October 20th, 1928

---

[29] [The Margherita House is an observatory now belonging to the Italian Alpine House. It was previously used as a lookout during WWI and WWII. It is in Fontevivo, which is a comune in the Province of Parma.]

Preface by Cristoforo Baseggio

Second Edition

After the vast consensus and sympathies obtained by the publication of *The Death Company*, I would have found it superfluous to add more text to this second corrected and revised edition. I felt the need to exonerate my modest work from an accusation that could seem justified to those who read my book, without them first fully discerning its true spirit and motivations.

With a grateful heart, I decided to publish comments and insight of high praise from many prominent men and colleagues in this second edition. They are meant to give more credit and better emphasis to what I have sincerely and objectively written in both the previous and current editions. I will refer my critics to these comments, who, being incapable of finding anything else, want to expose in my book a style too personal and sectarian. I refuse to even pay attention to their accusations of immodesty, for it is not in my character and is not one of the goals of the book, which I clearly outlined in the preface of the first edition. The truth is that I had to speak highly of myself, despite my better judgement, to prove the worthiness of my men. In that era, from the creation to the disbanding of my company, there was no talk of arditismo or organic[30] Arditi formations. This made speaking about the deeds of my company a personal duty. I also pride myself on the approval of a high-ranking officer, who wrote "the book is good, especially because it is true." That brief comment, definitive and decisive, was made by the Historical Office of the Major Army Staff Command from their Bulletin number 4, 1°, dated July 1929.

It would have been a mistake if I stayed silent out of a sense of false humbleness, in whole or in part, and had not brought forth the Truth.

---

[30] A military unit that is a permanent part of a larger unit and (usually) provides some specialized capability to that parent unit.

It is the driving force that has always guided me in my actions and is the only real merit of this book.

Cristoforo Baseggio
Milan, July 12th, 1929

Major Cristoforo Baseggio

Acclaim and Reviews

First Aide-de-Camp General's Office of His Majesty the King

N. 943 Rome, March 3rd, 1929, VII

To Mr. Eng. Cristoforo Baseggio, Milan

I had the honor of handing His Majesty the King a copy of *The Death Company* you so desired to have him receive as a gift.

The Sovereign Augustus, accepting with much delight this courteous delivery, consented to assign me the expression of his best thanks, that I have the privilege of sharing with you.

Esteemed Regards,

Asinari Di Bernezzo

The First Aide-de-Camp General,

Assigned Brigade General

First Aide to His Royal Majesty the Prince of Piedmont

Turin, February 28th, 1929

Dear Baseggio,

I delivered to His Royal Majesty the Prince of Piedmont your book *The Death Company*, a loyal and lively recounting of the exploits accomplished by your brave maniple from the Sugana Valley[31] in the years 1915–1916. The Prince Augustus has given me the welcome assignment of thanking you very much for the gentle thought and for the much-appreciated tribute. I will allow myself to unite my most

---

[31] [The Val Sugana, or Sugana Valley, is a crucial strategic area in the Trentino region. It connects the Adriatic Sea to Germany and Austria. It is possible to easily reach the Brenner Pass following the Via Claudia Augusta, roads laid in antiquity by the Romans.]

humble thanks with the previous, humble but warmest, as warm as your memories are of war which are related in your book. And with that, have yourself a courteous handshake.

Ever yours *M. Aff*,[32]

A. Clerici

Telegram
Eng. C. Baseggio

Corso Roma 42, Milan

ST MILAN ROME NRO 65 24 7 15 | 15

8794 S. E. The Head of State wishes that his best thanks arrive to you for the courteous gift. Stop.

Party Secretary Chiavolini

IV Zone Command
The Lieutenant Commander General

Verona, March 6th, 1929, VII

Dear Baseggio,

I have received your wonderful book. It is a dutiful tribute of gratitude to the many valiant men, who generously gave their lives or made tatters of their bodies, and to all candid souls who gave themselves up for the great cause. You have written an honorable page in the history of the Italian Army. You have done well to write it. You have also given an *original* and *true* document pertaining to the history of the Great War.

It is exceedingly difficult to find authentic sources who answer to objective truth, and I do believe those responsible in the General Major Army Staff should be thankful. Reading chapter after chapter, I consider the various actions and think, how many times did I say, "if Baseggio's spirit had dwelled in every officer at the head of those grand units, how much shorter would the war have been and how much less the sum of sacrifices for victory!"

I do not remember if I ever wrote to you that last summer with the

---

[32] [*Affettuosissimo*, meaning "most affectionate" or "most affectionately."]

Cohorts[33] of the Forty-First Legion. We carried out the attack and defense of the Palù Pass along with the neighboring crossings, moving a Cohort from Borgo to the zone near Mount Salubio and another from Pergine to the Moncheni Valley and the village of Palù. I have experienced firsthand how opportune the direction of the offensive you chose was with the occupation of Mount Collo, and how easy it would have been at that time to concentrate between Palù and Cadino's Pass, preventing and foiling the incipient development of the Strafe Expedition.[34]

Kind regards from your *Aff.*^{MO},[35]
Andrea Graziani

House of Representatives

Milan, May 7th, 1929, A. VII E. F.

To the Illustrious Mr. Maj. Baseggio Cav. Cristoforo

Corso Roma 42, Milan

Dearest Major,
I have received your book, *The Death Company*, and I thank you for the much-appreciated gift.

I have skimmed the nice pages that talk of the first *Fiamme Nere*,[36] and, yet again, the heroism of your Death Company has appeared to me in all its awe-inspiring greatness.

Reading the pages of your book makes one feel taken by a profound

---

[33] A military unit of a Roman legion generally composed of 480 soldiers. It is typically about the same size as a modern battalion.

[34] Nickname for the Battle of Asiago. It was a massive surprise counteroffensive launched by the Austro-Hungarians on May 15th, 1916. The Italian Army was able to repel the attack and regain ground. With Russia moving onto Austrian soil on June 4th, 1916, the Austro-Hungarians were forced to leave their positions during the battle to respond. Italy was able to gain the advantage in the offensive.

[35] Another way of writing "most affectionate" or most affectionately."

[36] [Meaning "Black Flames." This term was used for the Arditi companies after their official recognition and change of insignia colors to black.]

sense of admiration for this wonderful youth, while the innate pride of every Italian cheers unequivocally the heroic feats done in the name of Italy.

Thank you again and most courteous salutations.

Avv. Gigi Lanfranconi

Ceglie (Bari), May 11th, 1929, A. VII

Dearest Mr. Major,

It is me, the voice of one of your most humble and loyal soldiers that deserves, if nothing else, to be heard because of the sincere admiration that I hold for you.

I have received your work. Is it possible for me to write a review? No. Firstly, I am incapable. Secondly, your intellectual and wartime merits are undisputed. Thirdly, even if I were capable of it, I would not do it. That is how much respect I have towards you. What should I say? A thousand different things. Have I read your work? Both yes and no! How many times I do not know! I greedily relived the joy of those good times in the Sugana Valley. The gluttony of both admiration and fear I have for you again consumed me, just like when you both praised and punished me during the war. All these factors made me read the book, skipping chapters, and then I read it all again. Later, I went down to the pharmacy to show all my friends, and then…a cousin of mine took the book!

Why, you must be asking yourself, so much spiritual pleasure? Ignoring other reasons, even I, who did not have the good fortune of belonging to the Baseggio Company, learned from the lively voice of the few survivors the glory and the feats of the disbanded company. I did have the honor of serving under you during my time in the Jonio Brigade.[37]

Lieutenant Rasi, the *Guardia di Finanza*[38] Caddeo, and many more

---

[37] Part of the Thirteenth Infantry Division. The "Jonio" Brigade was made up of the 221st and 222nd Infantry Regiments and was led by General Andrea Graziani. Captain Baseggio was also an officer in the brigade. The brigade fought in the Battle of Caporetto from October 24th–November 19th, 1917 against the German and Austro-Hungarian armies.

[38] ["Customs Officer" or "Financial Police."] See note for "Finanzieri."

spoke daily of the epic days of the first Death Company. Do you remember, sir Major? Lieutenant Rasi was the Ordinance Officer for the Brigade and Caddeo was the typist. We often came to greet you and other survivors from whom we learned of your work in the glorious Baseggio Company.

Therefore, Sir Major, regardless of other reasons, like having almost lived with the Arditi Company Baseggio, it has given me immense pleasure reading and rereading in your book the facts and deeds in the Sugana Valley.

I remember when you led and directed, with energy and care, the highly organized retreat on the Maso Torrent. I still remember that I was your most loyal soldier. I always followed behind you with a briefcase! That day, an entire platoon of soldiers, on your command, was made to turn around and fetch a case of abandoned cartridges. Your dedication was unparalleled.

In your book, the preface of the honorable Borelli, known in Italy for his patriotism and culture, is of extraordinary eloquence!

Who could, and would, say more and better?

After all, sir Major, let me say that whatever review, whatever judgment is made, it will not ever equal your innumerable merits!

L'ardito Caddeo

Lieutenant Guido Rasi

If I did not have sons, sir Major, I would go with you to do even the humblest of services, just so I could be near you to learn and improve!

I hope God will let me meet you in the future, so that you can measure for yourself how much deference and respect I hold for you. And with this certainty, I assure you of my obedience and devotion.

Dev.*MO*,[39]

Sisto Giuseppe

Il Popolo d'Italia ### Historical Biography Office

Milan, May 4th, 1929, VII

Dear Baseggio,

Your gift, from one Ardito to another Ardito, arrives to me most welcome. It is my duty to tell you that I did not expect a work so complete and well documented and still warm with the love that in war becomes the very breathable air itself, and in peace the masculinity of life. The greatness of this book is indeed in the formula that is at the head of it: "I would rather break my forehead than bend my back."

For the rest, that I will read. There is not much to think about other than the past, in which every one of us, now that the machine gun bursts have stopped, can find pieces of themselves.

I am incredibly grateful for the heroic immersion your reading offers me, and to this gratitude I add my courteousness and my utmost consideration.

Consider me yours,
Mario Dei Gaslini

---

[39] [*Devotissimo*, meaning "Most Devoted."]

Port Medic

Catania, May 14th, 1929

Dear Baseggio,

I have received your recent publication, and as a modest and elderly follower (so as not to say oldest in the company), I thank you in the name of all the survivors, the absent and the ignored.

Our sacrifice, previously underappreciated by the masses of combatants, has been artificially ignored in the post-war period. The true factors and the authentic valor that led us to Vittorio Veneto[40] were overshadowed by the tradesmen of politics and the exploiters of war.

After all, it was the temperament of the company to give all and ask for nothing in return. In doing so, none of us could have been highly valued in the modern race of super-patriotism, cold and *ventraiolo*.[41]

Nonetheless, this has not shaken our faith. I can guarantee that our friends of yesterday and today will be the loyalists of tomorrow at the sound of the first cannon's thunder.

A hug from your Aff.[MO],
Signorelli

Letter from Sergeant Vida

Dearest Sir Major C. Baseggio,

Before thanking you, I wanted to read the book. I lived an entire night in ecstasy and with the sensation that I was still there. I confess, I enjoyed certain parts where I had a say, and I cried the most remembering Galante, Galluzzo, Umerini, Vismara, Divina, etc. Good job, Major! This is the best reward for us modest soldiers, everywhere and always ready at every age, and it is the best memory that we could leave to our sons. Thank you so much. I will repeat to you, heroic officer, a phrase that I wrote in Strigno to my brother-in-law, as I had

---

[40] City in the Province of Treviso, in northeast Italy, between the Piave and Livenza rivers. The Battle of Vittorio Veneto (October 24th–November 3rd, 1918) was a major Italian victory and contributed to the end of the First World War on November 11th, 1918.

[41] [Of Sicilian derivation, this word is used for the job title of those who gutted animals and later sold their intestines at the market.]

just returned from Mount Collo: "Baseggio is the second Garibaldi."[42] The Medal of Honor most desired for us now is your remembrance and your demonstration of affection.

As a soldier, I will always be at your command.

Your Dev.[MO] ex-Sergeant,
Dante Vida

Sergeant Dante Vida

---

[42] Giuseppe Garibaldi (1807–1882) was an Italian patriot and soldier of the Risorgimento. He was a republican who conquered Sicily and Naples with his guerrilla Red Shirts. He contributed to the achievement of Italian unification under the royal house of Savoy in the mid-nineteenth century.

Il Popolo d'Italia
The Director

Milan, March 2nd, 1929, VII

Illustrious Major,

I have received your book on *The Death Company*. I thank you very much for the courteous thought. I will certainly not forget to read your volume with interest, which reminds one of this heroic time in our War.

I give you my most courteous greetings,
Arnaldo Mussolini
The Director

Municipality of Monselice
The Head Secretary

May 10th, 1929, VII

Esteemed Sir Major,

Yesterday, I received the copy that you have so kindly sent me. It is superfluous of me to tell you about the jolts I felt in recalling many memories.

I wanted to run to Milan right way to see you again and give you a kiss.

It pains me so, as I have already told you, to see you cast aside. Today, we see the triumph of one who has given most in a time of war, for ardimento and for intelligence.

With ever more devotion and affection,
Your Lieutenant G. Rasi

Venice, March 9th, 1929

Sir Major,

Heartfelt thanks for the magnificent inscription that you have addressed to me in the book *The Death Company*. I find it well compiled, with just a few errors and some additions that could be corrected in another edition. For example, Giovanni Gugusi fell on Mount Collo. He was shot in the forehead in February 1916 and was buried in the cemetery of Strigno. He was born in Fonni, Nuoro Province. He came from the Seventh Battalion on October 27th, 1915. The chef that talked was not called Gnocchi, but rather Impiccini. He was a lively Abruzzese,[43] a valiant Alpino. It was forgotten that Turrin the Alpino, who was wounded at Saint Osvaldo, refused medical treatment, even with a part of his head bashed in. There are other particularities which are probably best not forgotten.

Appreciate my best wishes and regards.

From your *Espl. Vol.*,[44]
Caddeo Sannia

Rasai, May 31st, 1929

Esteemed Sir Major,

I come with these few lines to thank you for the nice memento that you have sent me. I appreciate it very much. I say this truly: I have an obligation to you for having given me a memory of war because, sir Major, I have not yet received any diploma, medal, or war cross. I only have my old resignation from the Seventh Regiment Alpini. It is very pleasing to have memoirs such as these for their own sake. I thank you with much esteem and I salute you.

Your devoted soldier,
Secco Antonio

---

[43] Native of the Abruzzo region of Italy.
[44] [Volunteer Explorer.]

Avv. V. Enzo Ferrari

Milan, April 12th, 1929

Esteemed Sir. Cav. Eng. Cristoforo Baseggio

Corso Roma 42, Milan

Dear and illustrious friend,

Returning to my office, I found your envelope.

I return at once the newspapers and the letter strips you have given to me.

I will hold onto the *Curriculum Vitae*,[45] since keeping in my papers a document of such superb energy, activity, valor, and individual sacrifice is very dear to me.

I have not been able to read it without outbursts of emotion. And so, I repeat to you, it would be a great injustice if a man of such personality and intellect should remain absent from the vital fibers of our nation!

I renew the expression of my most sincere and courteous devotion.

Your Aff.[MO],

Enzo Ferrari

National War Volunteers Association
Milan Division

Milan, March 1st A. VII

To Major Cristoforo Baseggio, Milan

Today we received your most appreciated homage, *The Death Company*. Congratulations for the fine book that brings together all the memories from those days of strife and sacrifice, which reminds the fighters, and especially the volunteers, that *camerata*[46] Major Baseggio was a heroic volunteer fighter.

Your name also reminds us of those sad days in 1919, when you were the organizer for the anti-Bolshevik movement.[47]

---

[45] [Latin for "course of life."]

[46] [Meaning "comrade." Used to describe a member of the Italian fascist party who owns its respective card, and in so doing, becomes a member of the "Camera" (political room equivalent to the chamber of deputies).]

[47] In the years following the First World War, a situation like that of Germany

The volunteers remember you, and in their name, I salute you in the Fascist manner.

The Section Secretary General,

Costa Vincenzo

Command of the Military Division of Novara
The General

Novara, May 15th, 1929, VII

My Dear Baseggio,

I thank you for the delivery of your good and interesting book, for I wished to read it fully before writing you this letter.

You have accomplished something truly deserving of praise, for both the tribute you have rendered to the members of your company and for the history of the assault divisions.

I also thank you particularly for having brought to light my humble action, so humble that it did not deserve to be remembered, if not for the spirit who inspired it.

I wanted to add, in your book you hint at a colonel of the Bersaglieri, who almost went insane because they would not let him go to the Rolle Pass. Certainly, you speak of Colonel Menarini. I will tell you that he and his regiment were supposed to occupy a position, passing from Passo Cereda to Fiera di Primiero. From there he could mount a solid defense, and in so doing, retreat towards the Rolle Pass.

As you know, the Saint Silvestro Bridge (ancient border post in Val Cismon) was destroyed. General Lenchantin would not fix it before the operation, so it was impossible to travel to Fiera by car.

The day of the operation, I had a motorcar disassembled, then brought to the other side of the river and reassembled, so that I could bring myself across the Fiera to maintain contact with the Bersaglieri.

---

developed in Italy. Communist revolutionaries, along with their socialist counterparts in politics, began to lash out against public institutions and demanded more and more reform. They were met with violent responses from the Fascists and members of the military, many of them Arditi, as well as members of the Fascist Party. All of this happened under the tacit consent of Giovanni Giolitti, head minister at that time. He thought he could control the Fascist squadrons after they had liquidated the socialists, which were in opposition to both the Fascists and the military.

I found Colonel Menarini beyond the Fiera at Iror. I talked with him, and he gave me news of his plans. While we discussed the defensive position he had to take, I told him, "Colonel, go on to the Rolle!" He was unsure of this, but I pushed him. It was far too much to be asked of a simple captain of His Majesty, belonging to a command that should have given the colonel some part of the responsibility if he had only been properly reprimanded. I insisted, still fruitlessly, until he asked me, "Is this an order?" At that point, I had no words left and I went back. He later occupied the position on which we stopped. Do you see now how that colonel lacked the courage to make the only rational decision in that situation? As he was left the sole arbiter in declaring the position on which he should have stopped, it could not have been anything else but the Rolle Pass because it met the requirements needed. If he had supported me, you know he would not have gone wrong. I know he acted madly later, but that is enough for now.

Thank you again and farewell.

A hug AFF.^MO,
Spiller

THE DEATH COMPANY

Main Narrative

Due to a series of complex circumstances in the initial phases of the war (May to October 1915), the First Italian Army was stuck in positions of passive defense. These positions contrasted with the spirit of the troops, who were longing to fight.

Some moves made by junior officers, inspired by a healthy principle of counteroffensive, were unfortunately reprimanded by Superior Command. They did not want to compromise all the complex actions on our north-western front with any disconnected actions. These reprimands, even if strategically and tactically justified, or even if imposed by superior necessities or orders, created uncertainty, and demoralized our troops in the lower ranks.

The Austrian Supreme Command had, from the beginning of its operations, prepared a retreat of its troops from the Trentino to beyond the Avisian line.[48] This was because of the logical assumption that the Italian Command had to act with arditismo to engage in counteroffensive measures to improve its own positions on the frontier and conquer the line on the Fassa Alps.

After some months, seeing that this did not happen, the Austrians decisively changed their approach. They reinforced their defenses and accumulated troops, armaments, and services. They created strong centers for maneuvers and reinforcements. They prepared, with strong resolve, a counteroffensive campaign that was to develop in the spring of 1916. Since the Fourth Army's rapid advance from the Cadore did not occur, we failed in our first surprise action on the eastern front, and the looming threat remained over us that our enemies were to occupy the especially important Trentino. It was a menacing offensive strategy

---

[48] Referring to the Avisio River. It served as a fallback point for the Austrian Army in case their defenses were broken through.

that, by succeeding, would have toppled all the remaining formations of our army. This menace could have been stopped early if current conditions had presented themselves as favorable as they were in the beginning of the war. If the troops of the First Army were able to continue their advance beyond the old border, they would have been able to achieve this goal. If First Army Command had recognized the urgency of the situation and the necessity to act quickly in June and July of 1915 and then was able to do so, the menace would have been stopped. Unfortunately, there were various deficiencies in the very means to do just that, coupled with the irrational order to stop the advance.

It is not my task here to discuss the reasons behind complex strategic factors and how they are linked to the general performance of the war, nor do I have the necessary expertise to make a critique of the responsible members of Command. I only wish to explain what First Army Command did. Their directives, from the beginning of the war, were characterized by a healthy spirit of strategic counteroffensive. This was especially significant because it justified the creation and development of the regular troops and the junior positions. After the first general discouragement, a certain reactionary spirit developed. This spirit affirmed itself with the creation of small departments of Arditi, and subsequently lead to the official institution of the major assault divisions in 1917.

Under regulations, the formation of reconnaissance patrols and sometimes regimental and battalion platoons were planned and formed. These units were made up of soldiers, ensigns and officials who dearly wished to fight. These units, in their limited practical effect, performed inspirational actions of immeasurable value to the morale of both the troops and the commanders.

In September 1915, I came in as a volunteer, after having commanded a Volunteer Alpini Company for some time and having led numerous reconnaissance missions and small firefights. I was resolute to do something that would truly represent my usefulness in the army and for war operations. I proposed, to General Farisoglio, the Fifteenth Infantry Division Commander, that an autonomous company be constituted to execute ardite feats and surprise actions, and to serve as either a vanguard or as reinforcements in the actions of other major departments. This would provide positive motivation and set an example for the troops who were not yet accustomed to the fighting and not as fierce as those in the Carso. I will mention here that the troops in the Carso were also rendered inert by the actions of First Army's Command.

I was well known in the sector, especially to the soldiers and the people from the Sugana Valley, where I enjoyed a certain popularity. I abandoned the title of Army Officer in 1898, after having finished my studies in the *Scuola di Guerra*.[49] I then participated in the campaign in Sudan and Transwaal, with the English troops, and in the campaign in Libya with our troops. I learned, through study and experience, that *in war, especially in the mountains, particular maneuvers and surprise attacks accomplish better and more formidable positions, and that the morale of the troops and the offensive spirit are the main elements for victory. Victory is achieved when these elements are hardened with prudence and by an unyielding acuteness in their commanders, who also know the topographical qualities of the field of battle and can use them to their advantage.*

My impatience was natural before the spectacle offered in our sector of the war. One day, in a trembling fit of rage, I watched as the Austrians reinforced and armed their positions that were before weak in numbers and defense. My temperament was unfit for that unnerving wait. Convinced that the trenches would be our doom, I maintained also, for political reasons, that it was necessary to spare the Italian soldier any prolonged positional warfare. For me, it was necessary to oppose the general discouragement with an antidote made up by some martial action, even if of little importance. Such was required to lift the soldier's spirit and bring him back to the traditional ideologies of our race, of war, and highly maneuverable warfare. It was also to destroy the myth that rooted itself deeper into our troops with each passing day, that the enemy's positions were unassailable.

My proposition was favorably accepted by General Farisoglio and sponsored by General Andrea Graziani and General Clerici of First Army Command. I was later supplied with more resources for the creation of my company.

---

[49] [Meaning "School of War." It was an academy for military officers in Civitavecchia. It was previously located in Turin, where it also served as a location for general infantry training.]

General Andrea Graziani

So was born in the Sugana Valley the Volunteer Reconnaissance Company Arditi Baseggio. This was the first time that an autonomous department of *Arditi di Guerra* (Arditi of War), was formed. Its actions greatly contributed to reinvigorating the sapped energies of the troops. It also gave Supreme Command the leverage to constitute, in 1917, the first assault battalions, and even later the major arditi departments. This, in turn, propagated the *arditismo di guerra* (arditismo of war) to the entire army, and was one of the most important factors in our final victory. After the war, the vanguard of that redemptive movement fully affirmed itself in Italy in 1919 with the defeat of Bolshevism. It facilitated an awakening in Italy of national spirit, bringing Fascism, the son and product of arditismo, to march on Rome and into a new Italian Era.

The barracks in Strigno

The Volunteer Reconnaissance Company Arditi Baseggio was instituted in the first days of October 1915 by order of the First Army Command in Strigno in the Sugana Valley. It was comprised of thirteen officers, four hundred fifty ensigns and soldiers, and equipped with a column of one hundred twenty mules. It was under the command of Fifteenth Division, which was administratively autonomous and independent from the Twenty-Ninth Regular Artillery Depot in Firenze and directly dependent on Army Staff Command. Its goals were to

execute ardite and difficult actions and take part in vanguard
assignments to reinforce and support. Any soldiers who made formal
requests to their superiors and were deemed physically and morally fit
by the Arditi commander could enlist in this company.

In just a few days, the company was organized, armed, and
equipped. A flood of soldiers of every age, rank, and section, from the
Alpini, Bersaglieri, Guardia di Finanza, artillery, and even veterinarians,
came to enlist. It was a colorful bunch that came with much uproar and
vigor, but it was held together by the iron fist of the commander. There
were even literary men among our ranks, such as Professor Casati (later
Minister), Professor Galante; journalists like Lieutenant Umerini,
correspondent for the Italian newspaper, *Il Secolo*; and distinguished
medical professionals like Dr. Signorelli and Dr. Vacchetta. These were
volunteers who came to us from the Trentino, defying the gallows like
the heroic Divina.[50] In solidarity and brotherhood came all these
volunteers of war of every age and every social stratum. They all
distinguished themselves in hundreds of actions and many of them died

Lieutenant General Angelo Farisoglio
Fifteenth Infantry Division Commander

---

[50] Lieutenant Divina was one of Baseggio's officers. He risked the death penalty for
treason by renouncing his Austrian citizenship and joining the Royal Italian Army.

gloriously. All of them were unanimously driven by an ultimate and healthy martial spirit and by a feverish will to fight and sacrifice themselves to achieve victory. That was the *Spirito Ardito* (ardite spirit) in each Italian soldier, awakened from its century-long dormancy.

The constitutional decree that was issued regarding the company clearly stated that the ardite actions to which it was destined would shortly lead those brave soldiers to death and glory. The enthusiasm was nonetheless great, and great was the faith that drove us. At that time, rewards and medals were not widely distributed like they would be in the future—a diminishment to their value, in my opinion—and the names of the valiant ones who distinguished themselves in combat were not published.

The Volunteer Arditi Company Baseggio was the first organic department of the war. The Arditi were officially and autonomously instituted into our army. The name itself speaks of the goals stated in the constitutional decree, but they are especially proved by the numerous war actions completed during the company's first seven months. Those most notable for their tactical results were the conquest of Montalon, the Glockenthurm raid, the Roncegno attack, the occupation of the extremely important position of Mount Collo, the conquest of the great trench in Volto, and finally the last and bloody conquest of Saint Osvaldo. These operations have all been cited in the bulletin of the Supreme Command. Through these successes, we gained possession of the Borgo Basin and allowed our valiant troops of the Jonio Brigade, led by the heroic General Andrea Graziani, to hold off an impetuous Austrian attack in the spring of 1916. In the Sugana Valley, the Austrians tried in vain to come up on our right and turn towards the Brenta Canal. If this had been successful, it would have helped support the great frontal action launched by the Austrian horde on the Asiago highland and on the Pasubio knot.

My main source of pride among the numerous war actions I led was that of reaching the greatest results with minimal losses. I managed to obtain this with a detailed study of the terrain and utilizing ambushes whenever possible, with the prompt and sparing use of firepower. Among the most remarkable was the occupation of Mount Collo, executed after a sixteen-hour march through enemy territory and during a vicious snowstorm. The occupation was carried out using the element of surprise and with very few losses, despite the numerous enemy forces and the great defensive trenches that existed on the summit and on the slopes of the mountain. I had the habit of following the brief, targeted fire with a rapid advance and assault, to which the enemy could offer little resistance. I kept my soldiers moving quickly and prevented the kind of demoralizing halts that subjected them to heavy losses by an enemy who has arms at the ready and ample cover. I sometimes took advantage of the pauses between firefights to give lessons to my soldiers and officers on the correct application of firing their weapons.

Losses were heavy at Volto and Saint Osvaldo, where the company was engaged in combat that required a force ten times that which we possessed. We had no reinforcements and remained alone and exposed to enemy fire until the company was almost annihilated.

I will briefly speak about some of our most important actions in the months that preceded the institution of the company. Later, I will expound on some of the most important actions of the Death Company.

The Austrian barracks in Strigno

The Conquest of Mount Salubio

August 16th, 1915

In the dark of night, the Eighty-Fourth Infantry Battalion was mustered. Their operation was to be carried out at 2:00 o'clock in the morning along a crooked gravel road that went down from Strigno to the end of the Maso Valley Torrent. From there, the column (four companies of infantry and one mountain battery) was supposed to, after crossing the Torrent, go back up the opposite side to a secluded woodland until they reached the rolling stock of Val Maso. They would then approach the eastern side of Mount Salubio and advance to its summit, which was occupied by enemy forces and protected by vanguard posts and detection patrols. It was a tiring, six-hour march that had to be done in fighting order. *The secret of success lay in the quickness of our approaching march and in the energy of the attack.*

I was destined, in the capacity of Army Staff Major, to follow the operation. As we arrived at the rendezvous point along the gravel road, I had with me my two loyal Carabinieri. They had accompanied me for some time on all my excursions and reconnaissance missions along the Fassa Alps. They were two good, young lads, with enthusiastic faith and courage. I introduced myself to the commander of the column. He had been my classmate at the Military Academy. He welcomed me with great courtesy. The operative orders were prepared by Staff Major Captain Spiller of Fifteenth Division. He outlined the plan for counteroffensive which the brilliant General Farisoglio had promised to accomplish in this sector. He was supported by the General, that old Alpino and determined creator of the Fassa Alps conquest. Mount Salubio dominatingly overlooked the deep depression of the Avisio and the Rolle Pass. This concept did not contrast at all with the general directives of Supreme Command. It aimed to improve our positions and allow us to launch a defensive action. That, in turn, might have led directly to a counteroffensive if the circumstances allowed it.

* * *

Mount Salubio was the last outcrop of the foothills that went down from Mount Fravort between the Sette Selle and pushed towards the valley of Brenta. Its extremities ended in the deep Maso Valley and formed at its highest point a prominent river. In the enemy's hands, this presented a point for maneuvers which put our possession of the Borgo Basin at high risk.

Captains Spiller, Mazzucchelli, and Baseggio

We no longer had to fear for our right flank because the Austrians had abandoned Mount Cima. Mount Salubio represented for us the first step to climbing the great barrier of the Fassa Alps. The objective of this counteroffensive action, although devised by General Farisoglio, Commander of the Sector, and by Staff Major Captain Spiller, was never completely actualized. This might have been because there were flaws in the directed energy of the action, or because the troops, not educated or trained in maneuvers of deep attack and not used to receiving enemy fire, lacked the drive and the tenacity to bring the action to its final execution.

Even if it were for some, or all, of these causes, what is certain is that such a magnificent plan, which could have brought us great success, lead us to grapple on the low mountainsides of the Fassa Alps along the Carbonile and on Mount Saluvine. We then suffered a halt that spoiled all the advantages of our glorious advance and allowed the Austrians to launch their counteroffensive plan in the spring of 1916. This placed an insurmountable obstacle in the way of maintaining possession of a natural barrier on our side of the Fassa Alps.

The fact remains that, for months and months, we found ourselves pinned down in unwelcoming positions that were dominated by the enemy. It was during this period that our troops lost much of their drive, their faith, and the impetus that they were animated by in the beginning. Now the memory of that painful action comes to me! The memory of a Colonel that was encouraged by Staff Major Captain Spiller to take the initiative and advance to the end of Val Cismon to the Rolle Pass. He either did not want to go, he was not capable of it, or he did not dare. Whatever the reason, in that moment, he lacked the ardire. He would only go so far as to occupy an intermediary position dominated by the pass, which did not correspond at all with the counteroffensive initiatives. Nevertheless, he knew well that the Rolle Pass was not fortified and was defended by only a few corps of rear-guard. The lack of ardire and the inaction of this commander inevitably lost us that pass. It later became vital to the success of our tenacious efforts and would cost us many good soldiers. Alas, they were sacrificed in vain! If we had linked the ardire to tenacity, provided our first valiant troops with reinforcements, and advanced simultaneously on the whole front by pushing ourselves from the Cismon Valley to the Rolle Pass, from Vanoj to Cauriol, from Colle San Giovanni to Montalon, from

Mount Salubio to Mount Sette Stelle, from Mount Collo to Fravort and from Mount Saint Osvaldo to Panarotta, we would have found feeble resistance and the barrier of the Fassa Alps would have easily fallen into our hands. The tides of war would have been vastly different from what we went up against in the following spring.

Spiller, Baseggio, and Mazzucchelli

* * *

At dawn on August 16th, after a silent and orderly march without incident, we arrived at the meadow that lies below the last eastern peak.

While these operations were underway, we had a brief pause to eat and rest. Only a few shepherds were left in the alpine pastures. I still remember their hostile faces that demanded silence (we asked them for news of the enemy in vain). I remember that between them there was a bony hag that took out her anger on a poor kitten that was playing with her apron, and with a swift chop of her axe cut the poor thing's head off! "*Tartufel! P...'taliano!*"[51] Poor irredentism that carried us towards sacrifice and filled our hearts with loving images of those brothers of ours!

It was then that I saw, for the last time, the Junior Lieutenant De Giovanni. Just a few days prior, he had almost spilled the blood of one of his brothers-in-arms! Finding myself outside enemy lines with a squad of fifty men, I had encountered him as he marched on patrol towards Mount Cima with his platoon. We exchanged the usual compliments that are made between colleagues, but I rightfully realized that he was flustered and doubted my identity. Maybe his suspicion was aroused by the different uniform styles of my soldiers, who came from all areas of our army. They each still had their own uniforms and he quite possibly feared that we could have been the enemy in disguise. In fact, as he distanced himself from us, he prepared for a proper fight. It took trust and courage from him and patience and prudence from me, but I managed to make him stand down, preventing that brave soldier from committing a fratricide! Poor lad! He was one of the first to climb to the peak of Mount Salubio with a reconnaissance patrol, where he was struck by a bullet and killed.

Crossing the meadows, we were already moving deeper into that forest of chestnut trees that covered the first peak of the mountain. From this very same part came a sudden, well-aimed rifle volley that put the vanguard in disarray and threw the rear battery into chaos. In that marvelous moment, we saw the ruthlessness of the commanding

---

[51] ["Truffel! You, Italian Pig!" The word "porco," which means "pig," was censored by the author, possibly because he did not want to put such a word next to "Italian."]

captain of that battery (it pains me to not remember his name). He was a handsome man, blonde, tall, fit, and of few words. Having put the men and animals in line, placed the cannons, and without worrying at all for his escort, who was in that moment immobilized, he immediately unleashed a lively barrage of machine gun fire and shrapnel against the crest of the enemy position. Then, he managed to hold his own against the opposing forces and drove them back to their positions.

I had brought myself to the most extreme left flank to re-climb the eastern ridge, and from there I managed to recognize the enemy position and assist in the development of this sudden action. I then realized just how much our infantrymen were unprepared to fight, how much the special and elite divisions, who were first to attack the enemy positions, needed the firm demeanor of good officers to teach them to push forward and attack. It was in at that moment that I began to first conceptualize instituting an Arditi department for that very purpose.

Seeing the grave danger that threatened the battery, now without an escort and in too close contact with the enemy, I hurriedly got down from my observation spot and I dedicated myself to rounding up and ordering forward a few stragglers, who more than willingly obeyed me. I formed up a large squad and posted them in an advantageous position and ordered a counterattack with rifle barrages on the enemy that threatened and molested our battery. The captain of the battery warmly thanked me and proceeded with his heavy barrages, working to dismantle the mountain ridge and the adversary trenches to allow the advance of our battalion.

Meanwhile, the unit commander, having reorganized his vanguard and ordering most of his troops forward, removed his men from enemy fire and brought himself towards the left ridge. Under the cover of thick woods, he prepared to launch an attack that way. It was a longer, but safer, maneuver.

I then brought myself forwards along that same road I had already walked alone. The uphill march was slow and tiring. The troops were exhausted, not just because of the journey, but also from the frenzy produced by the present danger.

Time passed quickly. It was already night when, advancing cautiously with my Carabinieri, I saw that the enemy, accurately pinned down by our artillery, was retreating from their position. I repeatedly urged the major to hurry the advance. Without hesitation, I pushed myself to the head of the charge shouting, "*A NOI!*"[52] and threw myself into the enemy trench. It was almost cleared of enemies. A few meek soldiers advanced with their arms pitifully raised up, screaming "*Bono, Bono 'taliano!*"[53] I took five prisoners and delivered them to my comrades, the *Benemerita*.[54] Then I met up with the major, who advanced alongside his troops occupying the position.

Night approached quickly. The last lights of twilight allowed us to explore the position and place our men strategically for a definitive occupation. Having tearfully put to rest the remains of Lieutenant De Giovanni, dead while jumping the trench, I had to suffer another five hours of marching that same night through the forest, accompanied by my five prisoners (they were the first and at that time precious!), to report back to Division Command the results of our operation.

After a few days, from a reinforced Mount Salubio, our troops managed to occupy the overlooking peak closing in on the Sette Selle. It was a momentous advance, and if we had kept at it until the crossing of Fravort and Panarotta, threatening their flanks, they could not have withstood it. Such an action, combined with a large push on the Rolle Pass, would have certainly collapsed the entire Austrian trench along the Fassa Alps.

Alas, it did not go like that. Almost shaken by the easy success, we halted! In so doing, we gave our enemy time to replenish their defenses and slowly create that dense web of outposts, reinforced with troops, of which many of our forces vainly tried to wear down in the coming engagements.

---

[52] [The Arditi's motto. An officer would ask "*A chi l'onore?*" (Whose honor?) to which the soldiers would reply "*A noi!*" (Ours!). A more literal translation would be: "Who will take the honor?" "We will!" Later, the first part of the motto was replaced by "*A chi L'Italia?*" (Whose Italy?).]

[53] ["Calm, calm 'talian!" or "Easy, easy 'talian!" with "'talian" being slang for "Italian".]

[54] [Referring to the *Carabinieri* (Carabineers).]

The Taking of Colle San Giovanni (The Maso Valley)

September 1915

I. Insult to Injury

It happened during the first days of September. On a cold and foggy night, I had climbed the *Forcella Magna*,[55] our last stop on the road to Colle San Giovanni. I pushed towards the hill on reconnaissance around those parts. It was an important link between the two valleys of the Cia and Maso rivers, and a natural step to climb the Fassa Alps.

Before the hill and its lateral ridges was the Alpini Cismon Valley Battalion, commanded by a magnificent type of veteran Alpino, Colonel Rambaldi. I passed some unforgettable days with him and his proud solders. I will always remember the names of the Lieutenants Palatini, Frescura, Ferruglio, Scoton, and Quatini, who were the most valorous among them.

I performed the first reconnaissance, escorting about thirty Alpini, led by Lieutenant Palatini. In my mind, Palatini immediately secured a place in the Arditi Company that I planned to create.

I placed the platoon on an outlying hill some three hundred meters from the enemy occupied position of Colle San Giovanni. While our platoon harassed them with its volleys and captured their attention, I pushed ahead. I stepped just to the outskirts of the enemy line, until I arrived behind it, about two hundred meters from a hut where I caught a glimpse of a group of officers. This led me to believe that a command

---

[55] A crucial peak for Italian forces, as it connected the backline HQs to the front lines and protected them at the same time. It was important to keep this mountain well-defended as it served as a launch point for any offensive operations further into the Trentino region.

center stood there. In that moment, I believed I had pushed my boldness far enough. I saw that the enemy was dangerously close to me and as I had reached my goal of identifying their positions, and noting their flanks and weaknesses, I decided to leave.

I was stopped, however, with an idea…

As they pointed their binoculars at me, I thought I would satisfy the Call of Nature and calmly empty my bowels. So, under the astonished gaze of the enemy officers, I left on the ground a little memento which I marked with a stick. It was my calling card, in clear view and with respectful greetings. In honor of Cecco Beppe![56]

Recovering from their astonishment, the enemy realized the mockery I had made of them and quickly started to rush in and out of that mountain hut. A barrage of rifle fire from the nearby houses immediately followed, and those shots made me beat a hasty retreat into the thick forest and down the valley, protected by the suppressing fire of the platoon of Alpini. They had witnessed the scene from above and had laughingly intensified their fire!

That evening I returned to Forcella Magna, satisfied, and convinced to try a *coup de main*[57] on the enemy position. From what I had gathered during my reconnaissance, it would have been easy to recognize their supporting positions and their reinforcing trenches up to the Fassa Alps, and then try to occupy them outright.

II. The Assault and Conquest

Under cover of darkness, Palatini and I left with a platoon of Alpini from Forcella Magna around 3:00 o'clock the next morning. We went down to the end of the Cia Valley, through the woods and around cliffs, soaked by the morning dew and exhausted. We crossed the Torrent, came back on the other side and, with the sun high up, we found ourselves in a clearing behind the enemy position on Colle San Giovanni. From this position, it was possible to study the trench

---

[56] The nickname given to Franz Joseph, Emperor of Austria. His name translates to Francesco Giuseppe in Italian. Shortening these two names produces the more comical "Cecco Beppe."

[57] [Translated from the French, meaning " sudden attack in force."]

entryways from the reverse side. I sketched them with much diligence in my notebook.

Around 8:00 o'clock in the morning we were favored by the heavy fog that extended itself over the mountains and concealed our presence from the enemy. We advanced quickly but cautiously. We immersed ourselves in the mountain's silence, turning wide from the hut where the Austrian Command was located. When I determined we were on the backside of the enemy trench on Colle San Giovanni, I threw myself forward, inciting Palatini and his men with the rousing cry of "Savoia!"[58] He ordered them forward and we broke through their positions. In the thick fog we could see the remaining enemy. They were taken by surprise and jumped like rabbits down the cliff into the valley to escape from our guns and daggers.

We gathered a nice bounty, happy and proud of our successful operation. After holding the position for some hours, we painfully returned to Forcella Magna that night. We had to abandon the conquered position because we could not keep it. It was too far out and exposed.

I never again saw the poor Lieutenant Palatini, who was a most valiant comrade, during those two days. He had so dearly wished to accompany me and the men in that forward attack. I learned that he died two days after, having been ripped apart by a grenade planted by the enemy at the feet of Colle San Giovanni. How many like him were destined to not be seen again and now live only in memory!

---

[58] The Italian monarchist battle cry. Soldiers shouted the name of Italy's royal house, Savoy, while charging into battle.

The reconnaissance on Colle San Giovanni

Reconnaissance on Ranch Palauro

September 1915

It was a sad day in September 1915. It was pouring. I climbed to Bagni Sella that evening, with the intention of selecting about fifty soldiers with Arditi qualities from the Eighty-Third Infantry. During the night, we would push towards the great valley of Bosco to locate enemy positions along the Carbonile and Ranch Palauro, which dominated the valley and were occupied by heavy contingents of Austrian soldiers. They protected this land through which their supplies passed, destined for the Sette Comuni highlands.

It was difficult to note the exact enemy positions on the Carbonile and distinguish them from those of the Ranch Palauro in the Army Staff documentation. Identifying them at night, during combat, was impossible. At night, in a wooded area that was broken, harsh, mountainous, we went along with hurried steps, trusting only ourselves, our instincts, and the darkness to surprise the enemy.

Ranch Palauro, even if it is not part of the so-called Carbonile, is in reality adjacent to it. And that explains why I, returning from Ranch Palauro, could confuse that with the position on the Carbonile. Yet, nothing terrible happened, as the objectives of my reconnaissance were met.

It was still pouring. As soon as I reached the Bagni Sella, I gave orders to the willing Arditi who immediately volunteered. Then I, along with Sergeant Major Melen, climbed up Mount Argentera to scout the enemy positions below and determine the best way to approach them. We returned to Bagni Sella during the night, soaked to the bone and numbed by the cold. We slept until midnight and then left our trenches.

It is not often that I meet a soldier more beautiful than Sergeant Major Melen. He was active, intelligent, and cunning. He led his soldiers under cover of darkness with the admirable skill of a few measured whistles. He spotted and studied the footprints left in the snow by enemy patrols. He ran from one end of the column to the other, so he could check and organize it. In a word, he was simply prodigious.

We had marched for a few good hours, navigating the land with our compass. We knew we had to be close to our destination, given the time spent and the distance presumably traveled. A sudden brief, commanding whistle indicated "Halt!" made us stop. I cautiously advanced towards the sergeant. He pointed out a dark mass with a suspicious ray of light. It had to be a house, but at what distance? We prudently walked a wide circle around it to get a better view, when suddenly we saw behind it many shining lights. For us it was quite the phantasmagorical spectacle, as we were not used to seeing so many lights at night. We had stumbled right into the middle of the enemy's position, possibly having passed through the vanguard lines of their lookouts without even realizing it. In front and below us appeared the Austrian camps of Barco Valley, from which they sent out reinforcements into the highlands.

While we were exploring the terrain and closing in on the house, I hit my knee against an obstacle that, upon impact, suddenly shook and yelled out. It was a sleeping Austrian lookout! After a few moments of shock, the man was killed on the spot, but his death gasp sounded an alarm and a storm of disorderly rifle volleys followed. We had but a moment of respite, immediately followed by a calm in our nerves and ready obedience as we heard the rapid and concise orders. In those circumstances, we especially had to avoid being taken as prisoners.

Making sure my men were silent and well covered along the ground, I gave orders to conserve ammo and to position a few spotters on the right, left, and behind us, so that our retreat would be clear. Meanwhile I searched—for that was our original objective—to discover the number of troops and emplacements of the enemy forces. I ordered Sergeant Melen to advance with two Arditi and try to ascertain what was happening inside the house. Strange and confused noises were emanating from inside, along with the sound of footsteps and hushed voices. Melen, armed with grenades, advanced arditously and, having spotted a window, threw a grenade through it that exploded with a profound roar. Shouts and whimpers followed from inside, while from outside a well-aimed volley hit poor Melen and killed him His two comrades were also wounded. I then ordered my men to open fire.

Taking advantage of the suppressing fire, I immediately sent out a patrol to bring back Melen, but another three valiant men fell wounded. The patrol was forced to return without succeeding in its intentions.

After several other vain attempts, the first gleam of dawn started to break the darkness. In the growing light, I feared the enemy would realize the inadequacy of my forces, so I organized a retreat. It was the first time I left one of my wounded to fall into enemy hands. I was grieved and saddened to return to our lines without him. There was nothing that I could do, so I had to give up, and took only poor Melen's cloak and wallet with me.

In the days following, a patrol of the Eighty-Third Infantry left from Bagni Sella for reconnaissance. They came halfway up a street near Ranch Palauro and found a note pinned with a dagger to an abandoned door. The note was later delivered to me. It read:

To Commander Baseggio,
I perform a pitiful duty in informing you that our valorous Sergeant Major Melen was buried here by us with all honorable rights.

The Dispatch Commander
(Illegible signature)

Even this action served to prove that in many circumstances of mountain warfare, the bravery and valor of Arditi infantrymen can be of help to the command in recognizing enemy positions, and that troops with an excellent Arditi education are needed.

It was through this and other reconnaissance missions, along with other ardite actions, that Division Command could ascertain the forces and positions with which the enemy reinforced the Barco Valley ridge between Ranch Palauro and the Carbonile. This was valuable to assist with the defense and protection of the troops and the assistant divisions camped at the end of the outgoing valley, towards the positions on the highlands of Sette Comuni.

During these first actions, I had the opportunity to admire the intelligence and valor of many officers. I am especially thankful for this, remembering here Colonel Rambaldi and his helper Lieutenant Frescura, with whom I had already found myself in friendly contact with on many occasions.

Captain Baseggio, Sugana Valley (1915)

Of Colonel Rambaldi, I remember the calm he had in guiding the retreat of his battalion, who had struggled too deeply under the Carbonile. With rare expertise, he managed to successfully disengage when the enemy was already surrounding him and threatening to cut him off from our lines.

Of Lieutenant Frescura, I remember his demeanor when I, in transmitting him an order, saw him leaving his cover. He was almost ashamed of staying safe while I was standing in open ground being directly struck with artillery. In one instance, I was irritated because a captain had neglected his duties and ordered Frescura to relieve him. I ordered him and his few men to oppose the enemy, sacrificing every man and every bullet, if necessary. He obeyed my orders to the letter.

A few months later, Supreme Command gave the order to Artillery Major Cesare Baseggio (of no relation to me) to attack in force the position on the Carbonile. On that occasion, given my knowledge of the broken and insidious terrain, I managed to be of help. I was especially useful in organizing the attack on Ranch Palauro and the Carbonile.

Baseggio in combat gear   *Lieutenant Frescura*

The Volunteer Explorer Company
Arditi Baseggio

October 1915

The idea of creating an autonomous company of Arditi, capable of executing significant tactical actions, that would be granted autonomy and almost unlimited material resources, had come to me many times before. I introduced the idea to General Farisoglio and Staff Major Captain Spiller, and it was definitively approved by the command of the First Army in September 1915.

General Spiller

It was known at that time that the Austrians had begun to intensify their efforts. They reinforced their positions and filled them with troops. They prepared road, railway, and telephone communications. These lines of communication were meant to assist with the accumulation of supplies and to put into place large-scale supply lines ahead of a great offensive.

I suffered and tortured myself over not being able to do anything! I did my best to handle my emotions by going on little ardite adventures, little skirmishes between patrols and reconnaissance. It was those same small actions, of little tactical value and little influence on morale, that I aspired to make into something of greater use for my army and for my country. I wanted to make them something more worthy of my fastidious knowledge and expert experience as an old veteran.

Little by little my idea took shape. In September, I went to First Army Command in Vicenza, where I talked with General Graziani and General Clerici. With their approval and best wishes, I obtained His Majesty's General Brusati's final approval.

In the first days of October, an order was delivered to me in Ivano Castle (Strigno) by First Army Command for the constitution of the first autonomous Explorer Company Arditi!

The company was, for reasons of logistics, combined with the command of the Fifteenth Division, located in Ivano Castle. Administratively, it was autonomous, and to it was allocated to the depot of the Twenty-Ninth Field Artillery Regiment in Florence as a mobilization point. Tactically dependent on Fifth Army Staff Command, it would, as the constitutional orders said, execute ardite operations, vanguard duties, explorations, reconnaissance, provide reinforcements, engage in surprise attacks, etc.

The company that took my name, whose organization and command was assigned to me, was composed of thirteen officers, around thirty ensigns, a little over four hundred soldiers, one hundred twenty drivers, a variable group of ensign patrolmen, two sections of machine guns, one hundred twenty mules, black uniforms, and all necessary equipment meant to render our movement fast and stealthy. We would be able to organize and deploy effectively and efficiently at only a moment's notice.

Throughout our actions, the effective manpower of the company was rather unstable because of the constant losses and subsequent number of volunteers, who came to join us after every action. The replacements were motivated by the enthusiasm generated by our victorious feats and driven by a will to emulate us.

I had gathered the soldiers of different units into six separate platoons. One was made up of Alpini, one of Bersaglieri, one of Guardia di Finanza, two of infantry, and one of miscellaneous soldiers. This was done to keep a sense of aesthetics and order intact, and to further encourage a strong sense of identity in the soldiers. Numerous officers and ensigns, along with the best weapons and equipment, were at my disposal to execute missions.

Ivano Castle (Sugana Valley)
Headquarters of the Fifteenth Division

The company presented a picturesque and singular spectacle. It was a wide range of soldiers from every unit of the army. We brought in soldiers of every age and social class. They were all full of ardimento and faith, all sons of our dear Italy, always tightly united to its banner. It was a multifaceted phalanx, but whole and solid in its courage and the certain faith of its good soldiers. They were Arditi; proud, cheerful, and always ready to jump into danger. They did not worry about the results of even the riskiest operations. It was rather necessary, at times, to temper their overwhelming enthusiasm. Ah, those impatient and turbulent Arditi, a restless collection of fine soldiers. Only my voice and my presence sufficed to make them obedient and docile like lambs, reading my every move, fearless in the face of the worst hardships, disciplined in their very substance even if not always in their form. They were good, loyal, and always ready to sacrifice themselves, not only for their country, but also for me. Everyone feared me like fire, but I was also loved by all as a father.

Some said they were too undisciplined and sometimes there were rumors of vicious looting. These were exaggerations and slanders spread by the lowest, most envious of fools. Never was a department more zealous in their duties, more ready for sacrifice! Hundreds of them enthusiastically gave up their lives for their country and for a sense of duty. Their turbulence and exuberance were manifested in the gravest and most dangerous of situations, but never their lack of discipline. If at times they offered no quarter or took spoils, it was always done by my order and was never excessive or needlessly cruel. A few chickens stolen or some barrels of wine emptied can never tarnish the pages of heroism written by those valiant men, and the meager loot taken was certainly not enough to pay for the blood spilled!

In their honor, I remember in Roncegno, my Arditi generously offered their aid to save the rich goods of its great hotel and the precious artifacts and works of art in Villa De Giovanni.

Cheerfulness was the prevailing note of those mighty who died singing and were always in good spirits. I recall jolly Bianchi when he was scouting the enemy terrain at night outside our lines. He encountered an old spinet[59] and carried it on his strong back all the way

---

[59] A small harpsichord or piano. They were extremely popular in the eighteenth century. It later became the most affordable type of piano for poor Europeans in the

to the cave he was using for cover. He did this, risking his own life, just for the joy of brightening up the long hours of waiting between skirmishes.

One time in Torcegno, a soldier found a destroyed and abandoned crucifix. He took it and carried it around triumphantly, with a childish joy. His theft did require a quick punishment to dispel any wish he might have had of looting again, but I could not fault him for his exuberance.

Confronted with these episodes of lively humanity, I deem them almost necessary to overcome pain and terror. Those proud and happy men, who upon finishing a combat encounter, tired and bleeding from their wounds, came back to our lines singing! They did so despite the forbidding, defiant enemy shrapnel that followed us fiercely from above the dark Panarotta! Their favorite spoils were black and yellow flags, binoculars, raincoats, cloaks, rifles, and bayonets. Yet, the trophies of war never distracted my Arditi from transporting on their shoulders, for miserable long marching hours, our dead and our wounded! Borgo saw them hundreds of times, the glorious returns to those patriotic people, who stayed in their ruined houses, eschewing danger. They have not forgotten the Arditi from the Death Company!

In October 1915, the company was fully organized, disciplined and educated.

Officials, ensigns, and soldiers of every unit of the army flocked in droves to Strigno to be assigned to the company. Offering themselves voluntarily meant we had some excellent elements in our ranks. I had accrued for myself a certain fame that was not such as to encourage the timid to join. As soon as they arrived, I submitted them to a sure-fire test, putting them on risky patrols against random enemy positions. Using this method, it was easy to make a safe selection from the volunteers. The company was now ready for action!

In the months of October and November, we accomplished many Ardite raids and reconnaissance missions outside even the most forward lines. These actions were meant to gather intelligence on enemy positions and the strength of their forces, while at the same time training my Arditi for future actions that would require greater skill and courage.

My men used many different tactics to surprise and defeat the

---

twentieth century.

enemy, including the cover of darkness, fog, wooded areas, cunning tricks, and any other type of strategy necessary. My patrols routinely left our lines, sometimes staying away for many days, and pushed themselves deep into enemy positions at Sette Selle, Mount Valpiana, Montalon, Roncegno, Novaledo, the Glockenthurm, etc.

I will briefly say that some of these raids, the most important ones, were all marked by the blood generously spilled by my Arditi.

The Roncegno Raid

I was invited to Roncegno, though I cannot remember if it was October or November. I was called to find out if the mansion belonging to Professor De Giovanni, the famous Paduan doctor, had been pillaged and razed and to try to recover the abundant works of art contained within. I left with the entire company and with my one hundred twenty baggage mules. We occupied Roncegno and the surrounding heights to prevent any surprises from the enemy (our main lines were in Borgo, five kilometers behind). With the mules in place, I set out to identify the neighborhood of the De Giovanni Mansion.

My men opened fire and the enemy, hidden in the surrounding houses and woods, retreated silently. Half went towards the Presoppo Mountains (from which they later tormented us with rifles and machine guns) and half towards Marter and Novaledo. I pushed two platoons that way with Lieutenant Pieri and Gagliotti, to engage the seemingly strong enemy force. With care for little else, I set about recovering what little precious things were still left in the mansion.

A pitiful spectacle met our eyes as we marched into that once cheerful village. It had been destroyed and plundered by the enemy. Suffering the same fate as all those little towns located in no-man's-land, Roncegno was cut in half and was victim to raids by both sides. Devastation and disorder reigned. The houses, gutted and broken by artillery shelling, welcomed us with a desolate air. Inside there was smashed furniture, broken glass, and beds ruined and overturned. Myriads of papers, cards, books, and objects of little value cluttered the floors and staircases. Like a river overflowing on all sides, the destruction went right into the street. Here and there were rotting corpses, limbs stiff in grotesque poses.

In the De Giovanni Mansion, the scene was even more disheartening. The traces of disorderly skirmishes dominated all things:

mirrors and paintings of high value were cut and defaced with bayonet strikes; chairs and furniture were ripped apart; everything was in shambles. Only a bronze statue had, incredibly, remained unharmed, along with two great tapestries of the Horatii,[60] dearly loved by Professor De Giovanni.

We loaded up our mules with these works of art and some furniture of high value that had not been destroyed. Having made the vanguard troops retreat with great care, we left for Borgo, where we arrived without incident in the evening.

Our return march was very picturesque, to say the least. The entire company walked alongside the long column of mules, heavy with loot, in broad daylight and in open ground under the whistling of artillery from Panarotta. All along the five-kilometer route from Roncegno back to Borgo we endured the wrath of the enemy artillerymen who attacked us furiously for the entirety of the trip. We did not meet with any grave consequences, and my Arditi were not worried. They were, as always, in good spirits…and full of good wine!

I later came to know that our righteously gathered loot, brought to Ivano Castle, was later delivered to Ojetti,[61] by Fifteenth Division Command, and later ordered to go to Supreme Command.

---

[60] Reference to the painting, "Oath of the Horatii," completed by Jacques Louis David in 1784. The Horatii are three brothers, legendary warriors, hailing from the Roman era. Their story tells of how they defended Rome from the Curiatii by killing them in battle.

[61] Ugo Ojetti was an Italian writer tasked with the protection of Italian works of art during the First World War.

Lieutenant Ardito Gagliotti

Night Raid on Torcegno and Roncegno

About an hour from Telve di Sopra (our furthest most occupied point in November 1915) lay the village of Torcegno. It was in a forest basin at the feet of Mount Collo and was where all the surrounding roads and mule tracks intersected. It was inhabited by farmers and lumberjacks. As the Austrian troops retreated after our occupation of Borgo and Mount Salubio, only a few inhabitants were left in the village. These were mostly informants for the Austrians and were openly hostile to us. They were the Austrians most precious spies. They alerted the enemy soldiers, camped on the forward positions along Mount Collo's ridges, of our movements with different signals. The enemy was able to prepare ambushes against our patrolmen with this knowledge. Our men often fell victim to the enemy, as they were inexperienced in that kind of skirmishing and not well versed in the surrounding areas.

Captain Baseggio gives the orders for the raid

I wanted to teach those bandits a lesson, and at the same time, push up to Saint Anna to find the location of the forward enemy positions. If possible, I wanted to disturb them with an attack.

We left our lines late in the night, after having merrily spent the evening on the Telve di Sopra. We reached Torcegno around midnight. It was a dark and cold night. Buried under the snow and hidden from sight by a thick cloak of half-buried chestnut trees, the village seemed to be asleep. Our entry was quick, silent, and impetuous. We blocked all exits. We had bayonets, daggers, and bombs at the ready. In moments, we had control of the village.

We made them give us the address of the Mayor and the Headmaster. Both were accused of being vehement Austrian ultranationalists and active spies.

We surprised them in their beds. We had them get up and we dragged them outside. There I declared them my hostages. Those two bastards were in for a rough night! I forced them to follow us until dawn to point out the Austrian positions. I even held them during the ensuing attack. That lesson, although hard and cruel, was beneficial and saved the lives of many men.

We quietly left the village, escorted by our two well-guarded "guides" behind us and followed by the pale looks of the terrified inhabitants. We made our way up the wooded mountain in a quick march, despite the miserable and dangerous climb through the frozen snow that covered the path.

After an hour of marching, we discovered a hut occupied by Austrians, that resiliently fired a disorderly volley.

"Bayonet ahead!" Without even a single rifle shot fired, we captured the spot and promptly set it ablaze, while the enemy forces quickly retreated to the cover of the forest and hid themselves to our front and flanks.

We had broken the first line of Austrian forward posts. We resolutely moved towards the second, having our right flank converge and keeping two platoons to the right with the task of keeping the nearby enemy positions in check. The march proceeded swiftly and silently, illuminated by the glow of the fires to our rear—a witches' Sabbath on a dark night—the whistling of bullets fired in a frenzy by an invisible and far away enemy, the distant thundering of artillery, and the silent woods around us.

The swiftness of our movement aided us and disoriented the enemy. The fire spread wildly in every direction, but fortunately it did not cause too much collateral damage. We laughed and walked with an ever-present conviction to continue wreaking havoc on the enemy positions.

Keeping tightly packed and in order, with many men having to hastily move through the thick woods in the middle of the night, was not an easy task. My officers and ensigns were alert and ready to accomplish this difficult feat without hesitation. My Arditi were already used to obeying and not one order was ignored. After the maneuver was outlined as simply as possible, I advanced with the platoon of ensigns and troops, followed by two platoons on the right and two on the left. The objective of this advance was the region north of Saint Anna. Two platoons with the machine gun sections and Lieutenant Pieri formed our backline. They had to protect our rear and flanks and destroy the huts and enemy outposts, then set them on fire. The mules stayed in Roncegno with Lieutenant Rasi, although he was dying to join us and was kept at bay only by my order.

It was a small maneuver created to be simply and perfectly executed, and it was a great shame that we could not carry it out with greater forces for an even better result!

We tumbled up and down the slopes or inside ravines covered in snow and ice. Sometimes we had to make our way through thickets heavy with frozen snow, with a bayonet in hand, our gaze straight ahead, whistling to stay close, accompanied by the sinister glow of the fires we had set. One, two, three, ten, twenty dwellings went up in flames that night. Always we moved forward. Around 3:00 o'clock in the morning, the entire mountain was covered in exceedingly high flames and dense columns of smoke that dizzily reached to the skies. The dry sound of the shots, the small explosions of the munitions on fire by the thousands in those huts, the gloomy roar of artillery and all the fiery skies made it seem like a fight in hell! Poor hostages! They had been following me under guard by two Arditi, shaking because of the cold and their own terror. I was starting to feel pity for them. I would have let them go, if it were not for the thought of our martyrs who had sacrificed themselves for us in those ambushes. "Forward, straight ahead!" was the order.

We finally reached, in the dead of night, a series of houses above Saint Anna, facing the Glockenthurm. We had reached the second line of the Austrian forward posts, after having broken through and left the first in disarray. Going forward now would have been insane.

Having gathered my men, I made sure none were missing. They looked like a hopeless bunch, made drunk by success and maybe also by the wine that they, the Alpini especially, knew how to smell out anywhere, as if driven like bloodhounds.

Lieutenant Gagliotti, my favorite and because of that the most reprimanded, even had his "coffee" up there, and well dosed with spirits it was too. Overcome by enthusiasm, he kept marching, even after my order to "Halt"! What a wonderful specimen of Ardito and Alpino he was!

It was there that I saw, in action, all the virtues of my good officers and ensigns. There was Junior Lieutenant Galluzzo. He was only seventeen, timid, but full of determination and faith. He was hesitant in the first moments, but little by little he became an Ardito, pulled up to this rank by my strong Alpini, who I had watch over him. I had given him to them more as you would a son than a soldier. There was the calm and smiling Rabajoli, always respectful and ready for action. The Junior Lieutenant Galanti was an artilleryman, an excellent soldier, and a patriot. He was a cultured professor before the war. There was Lieutenant Umerini, a journalist who had volunteered. He was already a veteran of the Argonne and Carso. Although he was young in years, he was an aged man from the many battles he had survived. Lieutenant Divina was a Trentino native and a most valorous volunteer. Next was Lieutenant Duke Casati, a cultured and serious former professor, always willing to expose himself to danger in any situation. There was the funny and devoted Lieutenant Signorelli, a calm, tireless doctor who served as a medic to the wounded and was also a sharpshooter. I do not know if he was more medic or more Ardito! Finally, Lieutenants Rasi, Pedoja, Ricciardi, De Lullis and the magnificent Lieutenant Vacchetta, both a veterinarian and brilliant poet. He was a most heroic Ardito. Among the junior officers the proud Sardinian, Cadeo, my right hand in the assault on Saint Osvaldo. There was Sergeant Artillery Major Banchelli, a veteran from France and the Carso. He was another volunteer, full of faith and ardimento. There were the Alpini corporals Bianchi, Chiodo, Turrin, and Durighello. Next, Tonon, Munerol, Vida, Solinas, and Spader, all wonderful and full of life and bravery. There was the valiant Corporal Vismara and many, many others. During eight months of sometimes harsh, uninterrupted combat, they all revealed themselves to be Arditi among the Arditi. They were always first to face any disaster, attentive only to the voices of their officers, and fearful only of their commander.

We reordered the company in the fire's glow and descended towards the valley and Roncegno, sliding down paths and frozen ravines covered in snow. I wanted to push myself beyond, challenging the enemy inside their positions, to get a better understanding of their defenses before the dawn of the next day. It was an audacious and dangerous plan that victory smiled upon.

The Arditi Turrin, Bianchi, and Ciola

After a half hour of hasty descent, we stopped by a house. From the slits in the window, we saw a light inside. I quietly called out, "Halt!" Four Arditi advanced, daggers and grenades ready. They broke the door with their rifle butts and entered vigilantly. Outside we silently waited, ready for action. They found two, poor ninety-year-old ladies in an abandoned bed, scared to death. They had stayed in their house when the population had already evacuated the village. There they waited, resigned to their end. We comforted them, gave them provisions, and kept going through the valley.

As we approached Roncegno, I ordered a halt and to seek cover as best we could in an abandoned house. Our exhaustion was immense. The thought of sleeping loomed over our heads, and with the day ahead surely filled with surprises, we needed to rest to be ready to fight. I slept a couple hours on top of a pile of chestnuts. It was not a comfortable bed, but my exhaustion welcomed it most warmly.

I freed the two hostages, offering to escort them to Roncegno. They preferred going alone rather than enjoying the company of my Arditi any longer. My young lads knew how to be "kind" when they wanted to be!

A couple months later, while I found myself guarding Telve di Sopra, a shepherd brought me a bouquet of edelweiss from the Mayor of Roncegno. Poor devil! He must have truly feared for his life and wanted to demonstrate his gratitude for having spared him. I did not hear anything from the teacher. He was more loyal to Austria than the Emperor himself!

The Glockenthurm Raid

There was a group of houses from the slopes of the Fravort and Mount Collo that could be seen from a long distance, dominated from a kind of castle with a tower between them. There is a rolling road that comes halfway up the crest of the Fassa Alps until the Fravort and Panarotta, and on that road is an incessant movement of troops and cargo. All this led us to believe that the Glockenthurm housed an important command center from where the front lines were reinforced.

Seeing how the location was far away and protected by the Austrian forward positions, as well as by near and far artillery positions, the Fifteenth Infantry Division Command decided to deploy a strong reconnaissance force.

My Arditi Company was assigned to the right flank, on Malga Trenca. Another infantry company got the left flank, on Saint Anna. A difficult and dangerous action awaited my company. Advancing from Malga Trenca on the Glockenthurm, we would have found ourselves exposed to counterattacks on our flanks and rear from Mount Collo, which we knew was heavily occupied.

It would have been wise to unite the two companies under the leadership of one commander. It did not go that way and because of this, the action was very disorganized and only my Arditi Company managed to reach its objective. Finding ourselves alone and fighting against overwhelming forces, our only hope of survival was to disengage and fall back. We did so, thanks only to the fog and our own bold actions.

At dawn on a cold day in November, the two companies left from Ceolina, one towards Torcegno and Saint Anna, the other towards Malga Trenca.

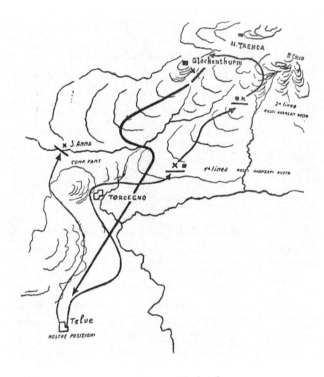

Reconnaissance on Glockenthurm

The infantry company encountered a small enemy forward position in Saint Anna and was pinned there until nightfall, exchanging very ineffective rifle volleys with the enemy. It was only thanks to our return from the Glockenthurm that they managed to disengage and return to headquarters.

My company was proceeding with a rapid march and about an hour from Torcegno, we clashed with Austrian forward positions hidden in the pastures that had been set ablaze by us in the previous days.

I took advantage of this opportunity to demonstrate to my Arditi that halting is often a significant cause for losses, especially on open terrain. In many cases, it is preferable to rapidly advance, even under enemy fire. In fact, as soon as we were targeted by enemy fire, I ordered a platoon to respond with only a few rifle shots and advance resolutely towards the enemy position. The enemy was amazed by this and began to unload fast and ineffectual volleys against us. They could not withstand our charging assault for much longer and disappeared into the surrounding forests. That platoon had less losses than the others that remained stationary in their positions under enemy fire.

I did not want to give the enemy any time to reorganize themselves. We went forward without losing time on petty skirmishes, catching up with the fleeing enemy in every direction. In doing so, we reached Malga Trenca with a few jumps from one firefight to another. We left the Mount Collo position to our right, and believed we had nothing to fear from out left flank, as the infantry company was meant to push to Saint Anna from there. I sent Lieutenant Gagliotti's platoon, and the machine gun sections of Lieutenant Pieri, to the right towards Mount Collo to cover me from attacks. Meanwhile, protected by the fog and the snow, I converged most of the company on its left flank and resolutely made a large front with which to face the enemy in the Glockenthurm.

The Austrians we had pushed back harassed us with small arms fire from the rocks above Malga Trenca. Fortunately, it was ineffectual, and we managed to proceed with our ardite maneuver unseen and without losses. The situation, however, appeared profoundly serious to me, and it would have been even more serious if I had known that the company assigned to Saint Anna did not push its advance beyond the first house!

It was around four in the evening, and we had been marching and fighting for many hours without rest, sweeping and scouting in all directions. Suddenly, through the fog, the unclear outline of a house appeared. I gave the order to halt and sent corporal Vismara ahead with three Arditi to scout it. Ten steps away from the house, we heard the brisk crackle of two machine guns coming from a well-hidden nest. Poor Vismara was mortally wounded on the spot. Another five or six soldiers were found by the guns and panic caught them all for a moment, facing the hidden danger ahead of us.

With a few, concise orders I hastened everyone to their duties. I put my two platoons in cover behind a small slope, turning back the frontline of the company towards the enemy that had meanwhile opened fire with violent artillery barrages and infantry gunfire.

My position was critical. A platoon with my machine guns was far away near Mount Collo. The company near Saint Anna did not give us any signs of life. We were isolated in the middle of the enemy positions that started to envelop us from all sides. The enemy, protected by the fog, knowledgeable of the terrain, and probably deeply entrenched, had every advantage on us. It was a decisive moment, especially considering the vast distance between us and our main lines. There was not much time to think, seek counsel or get help. It is necessary, in these circumstances, to understand intuitively the urgency of the moment and act promptly to face it.

I decided to fall back to Saint Anna. I sent orders to Lieutenant Pieri and Lieutenant Gagliotti to reach me, either in that location, or around Torcegno. When I started the movement, while two platoons kept the enemy at bay with their fire, my gaze fell on poor Vismara. He was rolling on the ground as a column of blood gurgled out of his throat. It was then I saw his grimacing and contorted face. He was looking at me as if imploring me for my help. In these circumstances, a commander must make a very difficult decision: risk his own life and/or the lives of his men to try to save a wounded comrade or get everyone away from the enemy and guarantee survival for the unwounded. Yet, you cannot always reason well in such moments. I dearly loved that boy that I had sent a hundred times before up against death. It seemed like a crime to abandon him there. I did not hesitate. I went ahead, alone and under fire, taking the dying man in my arms and dragging him low towards cover where my Arditi watched, astounded by the danger I was facing. I heard bullets whistling above my head. Instinct alone guided me towards the nearby shelter with the undertaker's prize in my hands.

To this day, I cannot explain how I survived. A sergeant and an Alpino rushed to help me lay down the now still body of Vismara. I called for the Lieutenant Medic. It seemed an age before he came to my side! I was overcome with emotion and anger and I reprimanded him harshly for being so slow. Poor Signorelli! He really did not deserve my rebuke. He had been helping the other wounded when he noticed three stretcher-bearers panicking and running away, so he grabbed his rifle and began pointing out their duties to them with very persuasive arguments! That was the only example of momentary panic in my Arditi. It was possibly a necessary incident, as those same medics behaved very well after that.

Giving one last look to poor Vismara, the medic shook his head and told me there was nothing he could do for him. I ordered that his remains be prepared for burial and brought with us in our retreat.

We retreated through wooded gullies that, along with the fog, protected us from enemy fire. Fortunately, our enemy did not dare to counterattack and only shelled us with their artillery. From near and far away positions, it angrily rained down upon us in a messy shower of projectiles. Against a sleek and mobile target such as my company, however, they were quite harmless.

Around evening we reached Saint Anna. We heard the crackling of rifles as we drew near. We were being shot at by our own forces! They had ignored our rapid advance and our retreat and mistook us for enemies, quickly opening fire on us. I had to move my men north, reaching our lines still under friendly fire. It was late now, and our troops were too tired to even think about picking up the action again and beating the enemy back from the Saint Anna advance. For this reason, having gathered and reorganized the company, I started the return march to Torcegno. We reached it well into the night, with all our supplies and our dead and wounded. We went back to our lines when we reached Telve di Sopra.

Even if the day could not be defined as a happy one for our company, though not by any fault of our own, the objective given to us was still completed in its entirety. Having put to rest Vismara's body with a few wildflowers covering him, we tucked ourselves away in the safety of Telve di Sopra's encampments to enjoy a few hours of well-deserved rest.

Lieutenant Doctor Signorelli

Sergeant Chiodo

Attack on Montalon

The mountain pass of Montalon sat on the summit ridge of the Fassa Alps, north of the foothill of Mount Valpiana. It was a natural passage that could be used to conquer the entire ridge. In the hands of the Austrians, it was an excellent foothold. From there, they could maneuver themselves, with assistance from the forward positions in Mount Valpiana and the Colle San Giovanni, to molest our backlines and any movement through the valleys of the Maso and Cia torrents.

The occupation of this Fassa Alps ridge would have also facilitated our frontal advance. It would threaten the flank and rear of the Austrian positions in Fravort and Panarotta, dominated by the Borgo-Strigno basin.

The Fifth Army Staff Command came up with the idea of a strong attack from the Maso Valley to the Montalon, to be carried out in two columns, with one climbing mount Valpiana and the other climbing the southern ridge of the Colle San Giovanni.

To this end, around five thousand men were assembled at the head of the Maso Valley. Many artillery pieces were given the order to prepare for shelling the enemy during five days of raids. This barrage was intended to harass the enemy and hide our true intentions for the attack.

The action would have certainly ended well if there had been more steadfastness by the command in executing it quickly. Unfortunately, the action was suspended without valid motive. It was later executed but resulted in failure. This indecision and subsequent failure was made even more deplorable because just a small number of the enemy were garrisoned in defensive positions on the Montalon. It could have been an amazing victory.

For five days, my Arditi had raided the region, creating offensive salients on Mount Valpiana, on the Colle San Giovanni, and on

Montalon, all the while studying the terrain for the most opportune approach.

We were in the month of December, with high snow and intense cold. On the day of the attack, all the battalions chosen to participate gathered on the highest point of the Maso Valley and were ready by dawn. The two main columns which were going to attack, one on Mount Valpiana and the other on the Montalon, had to be preceded by two battalions of Alpini. To keep in contact, a third Alpini battalion had to advance in the valley. The other infantry battalions had to follow in reserve, ready to reinforce one column or the other, or even the center, if circumstances dictated. The artillery guns had to prepare their attack in support of the infantry from positions on the left side of the Maso Valley. These were optimal maneuvers, but they ended up being executed with uncertainty and lackluster ardimento.

My company, ordered to proceed as a vanguard to the right column, threw itself resolutely ahead, crossing a foothill on the Montalon. Even if tired, my Arditi ached to crown their efforts with a decent victory.

After a couple of hours, the left column, led by Lieutenant Colonel Cesare Baseggio, came just a few meters from the trenches of Mount Valpiana without being spotted. They had been preceded by a battalion of Alpini, which had the valorous Captain Riva at its head. A hand grenade thrown from that trench hit Captain Riva right in the chest. Dying, he fell and dragged many of his Alpini down with him due to the icy terrain. This incident created a momentary turmoil in the column and this panic propagated itself to the backline troops who broke formation and lost ground.

From the other side of the valley, the troop command, scared by the vague news that had arrived from the front, did not have an exact view of the situation. Despite the lively insistence of Lieutenant Colonel Cesare Baseggio, they had the left column suspend its operation, and in so doing, they also stopped the other columns that had not even engaged the enemy yet.

In fact, the right column was advancing on the Montalon ridge simultaneously. Having marched through the thick forest of pines trees, they had reached the plain from below, about an hour from the mountain, having kept themselves always in contact with the column at the end of the valley. The news of the immediate left column halting reached the leaders of the right column, accompanied by orders to halt.

This was an incomprehensible and illogical order! We kicked snow around until evening and began to dig trenches to shield ourselves from the cold rather than the enemy.

I sent a platoon of my Arditi to explore around the hill and I received confirmation that there was more than one company of Austrians with a few machine guns in defensive positions, but that an attack presented itself as easy and advantageous.

I let command know this and I had no response. We remained inactive and more demoralized than ever until that same night when we received the order of a general retreat to the opposite end of the valley. My company had the task to remain in place as rearguard. After five days of constant marching and few skirmishes, we were irritated and exhausted. We still had our stubborn willingness to fight and conquer the enemy positions. Seeing the failure of an action so well organized for just a dozen dead in the first contact was, for us, humiliating and painful!

Lieutenant Colonel Cesare Baseggio

My Arditi were bickering now. They shook with indignation and would have rather died of thirst and hunger in that cold unsafe place rather than retreat. They wanted to conquer that ridge alone and maybe, if we had done it, we would have succeeded. I was too much of a good soldier to engage in an act of open insubordination. So, I kept my post, diligently following the orders received. Later that night, we received the order to retreat into the valley. There we found our tents covered by four inches of snow. Without even eating, I closed myself in my tent and fell asleep, still dressed, wet, exhausted, and discontent.

I was awakened at 4:00 o'clock in the morning by a soldier who brought me new orders to continue as rearguard and follow the retreat of the column into the Maso Valley.

I read these orders to my Arditi. I saw immeasurable disappointment on their faces as they understood that a sound tactical action was being thrown away, and what might have been an excellent chance to get a foothold for our troops in that mountainous chain of the Fassa Alps. It had been our dream for many months.

Then I had an idea, inspired by that sense of initiative that our founding principles dictated. I gave orders for a forward march and sent to Army Staff Command a phonogram with the following therein written:

Maso Valley Troop Command

During the night, my patrols spotted enemy scouts coming from the Fassa Alps towards the Maso Valley, who manifested the intention of attacking in the rear and flanks of our troops deployed in the valley. To better fulfill my duties in the protection of the troops, I will depart for an offensive reconnaissance mission in Montalon.

Captain Baseggio

I went without waiting for confirmation. We arrived at the foot of the hill in a few hours. We engaged the enemy and decisively pinned him, as he was clearly intending to counterattack our main line. We kept him there for an entire day, impeding his offensive plans.

In this brilliant action, we only lost a few men and carried out our duty to protect the column. We also gathered many abandoned materials as we headed back to Strigno after two days. General Farisoglio hugged me dearly upon my return and asked me if I preferred an execution by rifle squad or a promotion for War Merit. My choice could be easily guessed! Yet, I did not receive either one. It was not even necessary. At that time, there was no generous handing out of rewards and medals. By that same token, we never asked for them or expected them.

Occupation of Marter

February 1916

The occupation by our troops of the Roncengo Village, in February 1916, left much to be desired. It was dominated from above by the slopes of Saint Osvaldo, the Frattasecca and the Glockenthurm, where the Austrians held strong forward positions. From these, they could rain down artillery shells of every caliber, and easily go behind their offensive wedges in the wooded areas for cover.

In any case, we had to protect this village and protect our position with the more secure ones, on the Carbonile and across the Brenta Valley. Our advance towards Novaledo had to be swift. Our first stop was Marter, a group of houses scattered in the middle of the forest at the end of the valley. It was just a few kilometers from Roncegno.

A battalion of the Fifth Alpini had previously occupied that position, but it found itself isolated from our lines and was continuously harassed by the enemy. After some weeks, the constant disruption and casualties led command to substitute it with another battalion of Alpini from the Brenta Valley. They were reinforced by my company. I found myself once again in contact with the brave Colonel Rambaldi and Lieutenant Frescura!

My company arrived in Marter after an exhausting night march in the snow and extreme cold. We deployed as best we could in the ruined houses of the village, protecting ourselves with a large line of spotters spread along the nearby woods. I immediately realized the danger of our position. The hidden enemy surrounded our location and harassed us with numerous raids from their mountain positions and Novaledo. These raids were complimented by the uninterrupted barrage of 152mm shells from Panarotta and Frattasecca.

Life in that region was dynamic to say the least, and we spent the liveliest moments of the company's history there. It was only due to everyone's tireless work that we came out of that ordeal honorably.

Every day and night there were multiple patrols constantly moving. Everyone was always walking in the wet snow with no possibility to dry themselves, with low supplies, and feeling isolated. The only way we could let off steam was by drinking the excellent wine left in the basements. The Alpini were good company. Despite the distress and casualties suffered, leaving that place left us feeling a bit nostalgic.

I remember some episodes detailing the constantly good spirits of my Arditi, and I will cite two here:

I left one night to survey the spotters and went deep into that silent forest buried by the snow. There I thought I heard the melody of a piano that made me thoughtfully stop. At first, I thought it was a hallucination, but the sound persisted and grew more and more. As I carefully walked towards it, I arrived at a little house in the middle of the forest and saw a dim light shining from its windows. I advanced with my revolver drawn and spied inside through the shutters. To my surprise, I spotted the Alpino Corporal Bianchi instead of the Austrians I was expecting. He was sitting in front of a spinet piano playing the melody of *Vedova Allegra*,[62] ignoring danger as always.

I broke the glass window, taking spiteful pleasure in his scared expression. I then scolded him for his carelessness and ordered him to return to the lines.

Two days later, passing by a house in Marter where a few Arditi were hospitalized, I heard again the same melody of *Vedova Allegra*. Opening the door, I saw Corporal Bianchi, surrounded by the troops, playing his famous spinet. He secretly went to recover it and carried it on his back to our lines. How could I have scolded him again, that good Ardito who gambled with his life to keep the company happy?

The other episode was when Lieutenant Casati came with us as a volunteer of war, full of enthusiasm and faith. He always begged me to let him take part in one action. I had no idea of his capabilities, but one day I gave him the command of a strong patrol and ordered him to attack an Austrian forward post that had been tormenting us with sniper fire from higher up the mountain. I picked a dozen of my best Alpini and Finanzieri. I secretly gave a message about Casati to one of my bravest Alpini, a careful expert in mountain maneuvers. They left and I followed them from below with my binoculars while they climbed that

---

[62] Italian operetta in three acts by Franz Lehar.

steep and uncovered slope. Arriving some ten meters from the Austrian post, a great volley of bullets flew from the enemy position. I saw my men fall into disarray. I did not worry, as I knew they had a knack for finding cover even under fire. After some time, however, I saw them gather and descend slowly from that mountain. I then understood that there had been casualties. One hour later, they arrived at our camp and unfortunately, they had three wounded, two of which were critical. One of them was the Alpino I had mentioned before. It pains me to not remember his name, but he will always live in my memory. A bullet had smashed through his head. He was such a high-spirited lad! That brave soldier had immense courage. In labored breaths, he could only express his regret that the reconnaissance mission had failed, due to the decision to cross an open ridge. Lieutenant Casati had ignored the Alpino's advice, and in so doing, he exposed the mission to needless casualties.

I hugged him and wished him farewell, then had him escorted to Borgo. I later learned that he died in transit. His memory is dear to me, and I wish to honor that simple and valorous soldier.

The Emergency Expedition to Forcella Magna

We had just come back to Strigno, some half sick and some dying from wound infections. We were exhausted from the many days we spent patrolling with no rest. That was when General Amari ordered me to leave that same night for Forcella Magna, where one of our Alpini Battalions was trapped by avalanches and had been cut off from supplies for three days.

We left, like always, without a single complaint or protest. We climbed through the high snow on Bieno and Tesino Castle through a heavy storm. On the morning of the next day, after twelve hours of miserable marching, overcoming dozens of mudslides and gullies, we arrived at the feet of Forcella Magna. We did not think about stopping—there was no time—for at the height of the mount the Alpini were desperately calling for help. We loaded up supplies on our shoulders and proceeded to climb the last ascent, the most dangerous because it was formed by the enormous avalanche that had blocked the entire valley. It was a slow and painful job that lasted the entire day and night, but we finally managed to reach their position triumphantly the next day. Our Alpini brothers greeted us with great joy and immense gratitude. We comforted them with wine and warm soup, and we could finally rest and dry ourselves.

At night, we bid farewell to the Alpini and quickly descended into the valley. I had placed the mules in some shacks we had built next to the mountain. The entire company was grouped in one big shack and after a half hour of merry songs, tiredness won over and we fell into a well-earned sleep. I was quietly chatting with Dr. Signorelli before falling asleep, when a strange creaking of the shack made me suspicious. We walked out to check around the structure and made a terrifying discovery. A huge mass of snow had slid down and piled up right against the wall of our shack and was slowly pushing it into the valley! The danger was imminent and deadly. I did not hesitate for even a moment. I woke everyone up and had them get out of the shack. As soon as we were out, it began to bend and crumble under the strong push of the snow. A few moments later, the mass of snow slid right down into the valley and carried our shack along with it. It sped up as it went along at a ruinous pace until it plunged into the river below.

My men, even if half naked, were saved. Many of them were without shoes as they stood around me in the snow, stupefied by the sudden wake-up call and the danger they just unknowingly faced. Fortunately, the shacks for the mules were situated higher up and did not suffer the same fate.

We spent the night, as you could easily imagine, as best we could in other barracks already occupied by different troops. There we resupplied ourselves with clothes and food. Despite the many moments of discomfort and hazard, the return to Strigno was made in perfect order and accompanied by patriotic songs.

The Attack and Conquest of Mount Collo

March 1916

Mount Collo was a bastion two thousand meters up that was connected by a large mountain spur to the Sette Selle. It stretched out on the edges of an isolated and wooded promontory that dominated the Calamento Valley, the Torcegno Valley, the access points to Borgo Valley and Mount Salubio. It was covered by a thick pine forest and was full of traps. In the hands of the Austrians in 1916, it represented a formidable maneuvering point from which attacks on our flanks or rear at the end of the valley could be executed. In our hands, however, it could have been an important step in the frontal climb up the Fassa Alps, in conjunction with the Sette Selle and the Mount Fravort flank.

As we had occupied Mount Salubio in August 1915 and made our advance into the valley of Borgo, it was vital to proceed to occupy the dominating heights. Mount Collo was the first and most important one, only after Mount Saint Osvaldo.

View of Mount Collo

Up until then there had been many vain attempts to occupy it. The position was almost impregnable with strong resistance, aided by the harsh wooded terrain and constant enemy artillery bombardments. An uncommon offensive spirit and discipline was required for the troops destined to attack and occupy it.

General Farisoglio, favoring our advance to the barrier of the Fassa Alps, gave me the order to attack the position and granted me the command of a company of Alpini. The attack of Mount Collo would have required at least a battalion and a methodical approach supported by artillery. Attacking with only two companies meant that great cunning in the execution of a surprise assault was needed, with the ready help of backline defenders once we had occupied the position. I was convinced that without a swift surprise attack, I would not have been able to overcome the resistance posed by their defenses. I decided to act on a stormy night and left at 2:00 o'clock in the morning from Borgo, determined to reach Mount Collo and occupy it using the element of surprise.

The night of the departure, I grouped the two companies at Borgo. We passed the few hours of waiting with songs, dances, and happy conversations. We left at exactly two in the morning. It was snowing and for fourteen hours we slowly made our way without pausing. In the sad silence of the woods, we climbed through the brush of Mount Collo, thoroughly exploring the terrain around us to avoid any enemy surprises.

Lieutenant Vacchetta, the veterinary doctor of the company, was with us and cheered us up with jokes and futurist songs. He was full of enthusiasm even though he was not used to fighting. In that respect, he behaved like a true Ardito.

Arriving at around 4:00 o'clock in the morning at the base of the mountain, I had already given attack orders to my company when I was alerted by rifle fire from above and by a courier that told me Lieutenant Gagliotti had met the enemy.

Dawn was near, and I did not want to give the enemy time to organize in the face of a surprise attack. At my precise order to advancing without firing, Lieutenant Gagliotti ceased his volleys and with his maniple, proceeded to the shout of "Savoia!" Behind him I had most of my company. The Alpini kept to the left flank, where they held the enemy with their fire and in so doing, facilitated our advance. There was a real race to see who could arrive first and surprise the enemy. When confronted with our lightning-fast advance, the enemy turned his back to us and retreated. Blindly and ineffectively firing at us, he disappeared beyond the Malga Trenca towards the high ravines of Mount Collo. I then ordered the Alpini Company to advance side by side with my company and to reinforce our flank. That company was led by a young Lieutenant, timid and inexperienced in our fighting methods. He was stuck where I had left him, pinned down by a few men and only one machine gun. His inability to move forward exposed the flank of my company. Seeing Dr. Vacchetta next to me, who had just stopped playing his guitar, I thought of ordering him to fetch my couriers and with Sergeant Banchelli, attack that enemy position and free up the Alpino Company. I issued both orders. Eight Arditi, with their Lieutenant and Sergeant in front, jumped ahead into a rapid and violent skirmish. They occupied the enemy position while the Austrians fled towards Malga Trenca, leaving behind many wounded. Sergeant Banchelli was brought back in the arms of his soldiers with a broken leg, but still proud of the victory achieved. Lieutenant Vacchetta triumphantly returned, having passed my first trial by fire. I gave my respects to the body of the valiant Cugusi, who heroically fell in the conquered trench. I proceeded upwards, followed by my Alpini and Arditi companies combined. The latter had managed to overcome the enemy trenches and had begun firing from them.

That brilliant action cost us very few losses and gained an important position for our troops that gave, as General Graziani later said, respite to our troops and allowed them to "further the maneuvers of our division." This successful action was only thanks to my Arditi, who expertly executed all my orders and knew how to successfully apply my directives.

The following night was extremely hard for us. We suffered from stinging cold and the incessant harassment of enemy bullets and shrapnel. Hunger and tiredness tormented us until dawn. For the first time, I noticed signs of discouragement and exhaustion in my Arditi. Regardless of the danger of finding myself short of troops in the event of a counterattack, I decided to send my company down the valley to rest in an abandoned hut. I should have never made that disastrous decision! During the night, shrapnel hit the hut where my Arditi were resting, killing two and wounding fourteen.

Lieutenant Doctor Vacchetta   *Sergeant Umberto Banchelli*

It was around 10:00 o'clock in the evening and I found myself leading my company, feeling dejected, disoriented, tired, and with frozen feet. I understood well how it must have seemed cruel to those poor devils to command them to hold their positions. It is hard to fight isolated and quite far away from your lines on harsh terrain and in unfavorable circumstances, where you cannot rely on either material or mortal comfort of other troops or leaders. It seemed pitiful to ask my soldiers for obedience under those circumstances, but no one deserted their duties. During the night, there was a constant back and forth of tired and numb soldiers who tried to leave their spotter positions and I had to endure the frustration of keeping them in their place. They silently obeyed and returned to their positions. They knew that although I was unflinching under these circumstances, I was also suffering alongside them. I tried my best to always be the first to give them an example to follow.

The cold grew more rigid. Wind and hunger made it more painful. I passed a few hours walking in circles in a little dip on the side of the trenches. I stomped my feet to keep the blood circulating, waiting for our supplies and the comfort of reinforcements to arrive. At midnight, I received a phonogram in which I was ordered to proceed along the

Malga Trenca behind Mount Collo! My Arditi were resting in the valley and the Alpini had to make veritable miracles happen to get any rest in their positions. How could I have ordered a new attack in those circumstances, without being completely insane? I answered back with a phonogram of my own that is best not repeated here. Command did not insist, and they did well not to. My men needed rest.

Around 2:00 o'clock in the morning, the wind calmed, and the enemy artillery slowed down their shelling. I laid on a boulder to rest for a few hours, putting my head on a block of ice that I covered with my cloak, but my legs did not fit inside the cove. I would have surely found them frozen in the morning if my Alpino, Tessari, of the Val Brenta Battalion, had not proceeded to lay on them to warm me up with his body.

Finally, dawn came and with it the reinforcements. This allowed me to send the Alpini back for more well-earned rest. I handed the position over to the relieving platoon. Mount Collo was successfully captured by our forces. We managed to resist and hold that position until June, preventing the great flanking maneuver of the enemy for Mount Cima and Tesino Hill.

The Conquest of the Great Volto Trench

April 3th–6th, 1916

From October 1915 to April 1916, every action of the Fifteenth Infantry Division, particularly of the Arditi Company, was working towards the final goal of capturing the great barrier of the Fassa Alps. For this reason, the troops had to gradually proceed from the bottom up, overcoming the obstacles for each step and climbing from the valley towards the last high ridges of the Panarotta, Fravort and Sette Selle. These respectively constituted the forward positions of Mount Saint Osvaldo, Mount Collo, Mount Salubio, Mount Valpiana and Colle San Giovanni, all facing the deep valley of the Maso Torrent.

Subsequently the following positions were occupied partly by us and partly by regular infantry: Mount Salubio, Colle San Giovanni, Mount Valpiana, and Mount Collo, following a strategy of slow advance, rational and unrelenting. On the first days of April, only the occupation of Saint Osvaldo was left. Occupying Saint Osvaldo would have protected our defenses in the Sugana Valley and facilitated our next maneuver towards the Frattasecca Ridge and the Panarotta. This was the last edge of the Fassa Alps facing the Sugana Valley and the bulwark of the Austrian defense.

On the final days of March 1916, the Command decided to occupy Saint Osvaldo with a great force. They gave the orders to prepare and support this attack, with our artillery placed along the Carbonile and Saint Anna, and our offensive infantry lines in the valley pointed towards Novaledo.

Three battalions of the Eighty-Fourth Infantry, a company of machine gunners and my company of Arditi, were chosen for the attack operation on Saint Osvaldo. From April 3rd to April 6th, the attack on the positions of Volto and Saint Osvaldo were carried out using only three companies of infantry, instead of three battalions.

The other two battalions stayed in reserve and arrived at Volto only on the sixth day, after the dust had settled. Five days later, they would climb Saint Osvaldo and occupy it, finding no enemy left.

The night of April 3rd, the two battalion commanders and I were summoned to Roncegno Bagni by the commanding colonel of the troops. It was decided that I would start the attack with the three companies of the Eighty-Fourth Infantry, a machine gunner company, and my Arditi Company. It was poorly organized and not well executed on April 4th, resulting in many losses for my men.

The shelling from our mountain batteries in Saint Anna and the big guns on the Carbonile and Bagni Sella did not have any effect because of the terrain's slopes. In fact, the big pieces did more harm than good, as they came up either too close or too far. Missing crucial locations, they had no effect against the well-entrenched and hidden Austrian troops. For eight long months, my Arditi had ached to climb that dark mountain, which beckoned to us from above. Within us all was the conviction that we would have conquered it, no matter the cost in blood. Our enthusiasm was so great because we were finally given the chance to focus our efforts on an important mission to make up for all the past minor actions. My officers Umerini, Pieri, Galante, Gagliotti, Rasi, Signorelli, Galluzzo, and Ricciardi were full of faith and ready for anything. The Arditi did not need any encouragement, rather they had to keep their anxious will to fight under control.

Under the Great Volto Trench

This did not lessen our melancholy. That night in Roncegno you did not hear the usual merry songs. The soldiers passed the evening preparing to fight and sending letters home to their families. For many of them, these would be the last letters they would ever write.

On the dawn of April 4th, having left the medical camp and kitchen under a rocky mass, I and my company, and a company from the Eighty-Fourth Infantry, occupied a position on the Austrian trench's right flank. Another Eighty-Fourth Infantry company took the center and the left. Another two companies were left in reserve.

At dawn, our batteries had opened fire. The shells grazed the ground and flew over our heads, either hitting the parapet with little effect, or sinking in the soft meadows above and below. Meanwhile, the Austrian snipers, well hidden behind iron slits in the deep trench, rained their deadly projectiles down on us on open ground without cover. Many enemy machine guns positioned in the woods above and at our flank gave us little respite and we suffered many losses.

At midday, I decided to act with a maneuver of my own and put a stop to that infuriating halt in our advance, the effects of which would have been devastating for us in the long run. It was counter not only to my method of combat, but to my temperament. I left the Alpini Platoon with Lieutenant Galluzzo to face the right wing of the trench. I launched the Bersaglieri platoon on the assault in the center. If the Eighty-Fourth Infantry positioned nearby would have strongly supported our action, then maybe the attack would have succeeded. Instead, my Bersaglieri Platoon was pinned down on a steep, grassy field in the open and suffered massive casualties. Only a few survivors made it back to the lines. The rest got lost in the surrounding woods. Meanwhile, the Alpini Platoon was left to fend for itself in the woods against murderous enemy fire. They had suffered many losses and could not advance. By nightfall, the action was concluded. The attack had not been successful, and the losses suffered were catastrophic. I decided that on the next morning, I would leave two companies of the Eighty-Fourth Infantry to skirmish with the right wing and the center of the great trench to prevent the enemy from flanking. I was going to try to assault deep into the left flank, which promised to hold terrain capable of covering our advance.

The night of April 4th was sad and sleepless for all. Many were either dead or dying around us and the thought of tomorrow loomed over us. My Arditi could feel in me the strong will to conquer, at any cost, that great trench. The enemy artillery thundered uninterrupted. There was no great material damage, but it depressed and irritated us. I was annoyed by the defeat suffered and for the useless casualties of many young lives. Nevertheless, I was determined to act and overcome our inferiority in numbers, position and means with superior boldness and an iron will.

I personally did not approve of Command's decision to keep the other two battalions too far away and below us. I would have rather thrown them all at the same time into the attack. Sometimes the reserves are better spent in the actual melee.

I bid farewell to good Signorelli, who was extremely busy tending to the numerous wounded. I gave my orders to my loyal Lieutenant Rasi, who reluctantly took them, resigned but obedient. He had to wait below with the mules sent by Lieutenant Pieri, along with two machine gun sections and take position to our left to support the companies of the Eighty-Fourth Infantry. I passed the few idle hours left resting and meditating on how to best lead my small, but important action.

It might seem reckless that I, after what I said before regarding our situation and having only five companies to count upon, would want to throw myself again into combat. On one hand, I was in no position to argue with the orders. On the other hand, I had great faith in the valor of my Arditi, who alone deserved the pleasure and honor of victory. The very thought of my company leading the others by example comforted me.

I was not wrong. The three frontal companies gave us enough peace of mind by stopping any sorties on our flank.

That night I informed Command of my intentions. On the dawn of April 5th, I climbed, with my company, through the forest and arrived quickly under the left wing of the great trench where a reinforced hut served as a blockhouse.

The climb had been rapidly and silently made. My Arditi were all lined up with me in the center side by side with Lieutenant Gagliotti. I had requested preparatory fire from our mountain batteries and the heavy artillery in Bagni Sella. These had hit the trench squarely, but with an effect more morale boosting than damage inflicting.

As soon as we engaged the enemy, I had the batteries cease fire. They then began interdictory fire on the approaches to Saint Osvaldo. I prepared to throw myself into the assault without firing a single volley, for I had little trust in its effectiveness. Having given the order to my platoons, I suddenly darted out of the forest with them and jumped onto the green hillside. The painful spectacle of the dead Bersaglieri from the day before, who lay in macabre poses, presented itself to us there. Nothing more was needed to drive my Arditi. To my command of "Forward! With bayonets!" answered the shouting song of a hundred voices, a cry of pain and revenge! The enemy immediately opened fire on my entire line, but we were already too close. We did not leave them much space for resistance. Lieutenant Gagliotti, first in the charge, jumped into the trenches with dagger in hand. We quickly followed, as if in one single breath. First twenty, then thirty, then one hundred! All by his side we crashed into the trenches like an untamed river, knifing and bayonetting madly.

Not five minutes had passed from my first order to advance, and I was already giving instructions to storm the front of the great trench and pursue the enemy that was retreating in small groups towards the forest into the overarching hills of Saint Osvaldo.

They were also being followed by the effective fire of our artillery and machine guns.

The operation was a success, as I had predicted it. While my machine gun sections placed themselves near the conquered trench, aiming their guns at Saint Osvaldo, I began preparing offensive reconnaissance missions on that mountain, granting the enemy no respite.

These operations were executed with the utmost discipline and hatred for the enemy. With their artillery and machine gun fire, they vainly tried to disrupt us. I gave the good Lieutenant Gagliotti to the stretcher-bearers and went to examine the insidious wooded terrain on my right. Here the Bersaglieri and Financiers struggled relentlessly in their defiance against groups of marksmen hidden in gullies. There I saw formidable examples of tenacity and valor of those mountain troops, to which I render my respectful homage.

I was about to cross a small ravine to reach one of my groups engaged in a skirmish, when Lieutenant Galanti grabbed me by my cloak and warned, "Be careful of the machine gun, Captain! Do not go!" An Austrian machine gun was placed high up on the outskirts of the forest and cut through the terrain with its volleys, making it dangerous to reach the ravine. I pushed him away, shrugging my shoulders and jumping inside the gap. Poor Galante jumped in by my side, maybe to shield me with his body. He took several deadly bullets to the chest. He stumbled, turning pale with a sad look, and fell. He was dead on the spot I had him dragged out of the dangerous gully while I proceeded with my mission. My soul was now full of sadness, but my mission allowed me no pity or rest. I never saw that brave comrade again. He now sleeps next to his friends and fellow soldiers, Vismara and Umerini, in the small cemetery of Strigno. With the reconnaissance on Saint Osvaldo, it was my intention to study new ways to attack. I planned to execute a mission to take the mountain on April 6th.

Yet, I did not wish to engage in such a deep and dangerous action with reinforcements so far away. I took sixty of my best Arditi. Everyone so dearly ached and begged me to take them that I had to resort to threats to get them to desist. They all knew I would surely try to occupy the chapel atop Saint Osvaldo.

We climbed on the right of the woody ridge which descended from the peak of the mountain to the meadows of Volto. We were all driven by unmeasurable ardor, almost as if it were a sports contest to reach the summit. All around us, we saw traces of the fleeing enemy. The dead and wounded surrounded us, along with ammunition and foodstuffs left behind in a rush. The enemy retreat, although silent, kept us alert. A few meters from the peak, I sent Sergeant Dumini ahead with three Arditi. I silently waited with my men, covered by the thick edge of the woods. From our position, we could clearly see the winding enemy trench split in two directions around the mountain top, from which it lorded over every access point. We were able to study the position and I could prepare a clear attack plan in my mind.

Borgo, Veduta

Suddenly, we saw an Austrian officer peek above the parapet, and we clearly heard him address us: "Come on, Baseggio Company!" A moment later we heard rifle fire everywhere, only outdone by the bursts of many machine guns carefully placed on the flanking ridges. The bullets scraped our helmets, but thankfully we were all on the ground and well protected. We did not suffer any casualties. Sergeant Dumini, miraculously escaped certain death when he had exposed himself on open terrain, thinking he had been called by me. He came rolling down the slope with his three Arditi and rejoined us. I had my men crawl with their stomachs to the ground, bringing ourselves quickly to a safer spot below. I was satisfied with the information I had gathered. An hour later, we reached the Volto Trench safely. During our evening rest we began our preparations to attack Saint Osvaldo the next day.

The Conquest of Mount Saint Osvaldo

April 6th, 1916

The evening passed quickly as we prepared for tomorrow's attack. Within us was the feeling that it was going to be our final day on this earth. That dark mountain would prove fatal to us, swallowing many comrades, and making a mockery of others. Yet, this same mountain attracted us as a siren would. I had the unflinching will to conquer it, even if it was going to cost me every man and every round of ammunition.

Silence and discipline overcame the usual overflowing joy. There was no singing, no jokes, no laughter. With the enemy so close and the continuous whistling of artillery, we would not have been able to hear anything anyways.

Arditi and infantrymen worked speedily to reinforce the recently conquered trenches and extend them to our right, creating a strong rally point in case of the attack's failure. It would serve as cover for the reserves and machine guns.

Dr. Signorelli was busy tending to the wounded and Lieutenant Rasi helped him in this pitiful duty.

I wrote a status report to Regimental Command on the actions carried out on April 4th–5th. I also communicated my decision to execute the attack on Mount Saint Osvaldo on April 6th, using my company and five others from the Eighty-Fourth Infantry placed under my command. Its commanders were all older than me yet gave me the honor and responsibility of leadership. I asked that at least two support battalions reach Volto to help us during our attack or to rescue us in case of failure. I asked the artillery to unleash an intense barrage of preparatory fire. The hope was that the barrage would be more effective since the targets were more easily identifiable and less covered this time.

As soon as everything had been prepared, I slid into my ground nest under the blockhouse for some rest. Lieutenant Umerini, to whom I had given the command of my company during the action, was also there.

Poor Umerini! He had always shown himself to be quite skeptical regarding the company's skirmishes, as he was used to the great battles on the Carso. He judged our fights as having little importance. For the first time that night, he had a hunch that this would be the end. The ghost of Lieutenant Galante, his loyal companion and cherished friend, appeared to admonish him. Maybe it was my words that shocked him when I gave him the company's resources and some of my personal objects in anticipation of the coming battle. I also gave him some recommendations and directives in case I did not survive. Without saying a word, he transcribed my orders in his notebook and closed his eyes to sleep.

I thought he was sleeping, but then I heard him slowly crawling out, trying to leave our resting place unseen. Later I learned that he went to Lieutenant Signorelli. Fearing his own death, he gave Signorelli a copy of the orders, and some money to use to fulfill his own last wishes.

General Graziani and Captain Baseggio at Saint Osvaldo

At dawn on April 6th, our cannons echoed around the peak of the mountain with an infernal sound, and they managed to keep the enemy artillery distracted from our real plan.

I did not want to lose even a moment. We had to jump on the enemy, still enjoying yesterday's victory, and overtake him before reinforcements would come from Frattasecca and Panarotta.

I ordered the machine gun company of the Eighty-Fourth Infantry and the machine gun sections of Lieutenant Pieri to strengthen the great trench, support our attack from there, and oppose the counterattacks to cover our retreat.

I sent a company from the Eighty-Fourth Infantry to the right with the task of enveloping the enemy position on that flank. To my company, I gave the main attack on the right ridge already scouted by me. I placed the two Eighty-Fourth Infantry companies in the rear as backup and the remaining one was to attack the left ridge of Saint Osvaldo.

The action had to be swift and simultaneous, so the two lateral companies left ahead us. When I saw them at a good place at the foot of the mountain, I put myself at the head of my columns and resolutely made my way towards the peak. I did not leave a single Ardito back in the trench. I hugged Signorelli, Pieri and Rasi, with palpable emotion in the air as we went. How many faces of friends, my comrades in a hundred battles before, would I never see again! The ascent lasted an hour, and at 7:00 o'clock in the morning, the Alpini Platoon, commanded by the young Lieutenant Galluzzo, entered the first enemy trench after a furious hand-to-hand battle and took control of it. The other platoons followed the example of Lieutenant Umerini and our company, who after occupying the first enemy trench, started firing at the above lines. They took grave losses due to the enfilading fire from the lateral trenches.

I then backed away to incite the backup companies to advance and ensure that the two lateral companies were in support range for my control of the position.

It would not be an easy task to leave the trench and descend along the steep ravine, covered by frozen snow. Out on that open pass, bullets rained down on us from a hundred different places, the snow now splattered with the red blood of my Arditi. In three years of war, I have only participated in such a furious and tenacious battle a few times. The exploding bullets burst with a dry noise and made leaves and broken branches fall from the pine trees. The air was filled with the whistling of artillery shells from the powerful 152mm guns, with shrapnel ringing shrill and metallic, clashing with the sounds of small fire from the trenches. The enemy projectiles mixed with our friendly barrages. Our artillery had increased their range after our advance, and they hit the backlines of Frattasecca and Panarotta with counter-artillery shelling.

Near the peak, protected from sight and from the shots of our enemy, my valiant stretcher-bearers, immersed in steaming blood, bandaging those with the gravest wounds as best they could. Those who were only slightly wounded either did not desert their combat positions or they returned shortly after seeing the medic. I remember an Alpino, with a head entirely covered in blood and an eye out of the socket, tell us, with no regard for his pain, how he managed to jump into a lateral Austrian trench and after having thrown a bomb in there, opened fire on an Austrian soldier. Unfortunately, his shot missed. An enemy bullet then hit him, slashing open his face and causing those terrible injuries! He was crazy, not because of the pain, but from the anger caused by that missed shot. Grabbing a new rifle and having bandaged his eye, deaf to any exhortation, he returned to the trench to "make those dogs pay." I saw him later at Borgo Hospital, still full of regret…not for his missing eye, but for the missed shot!

I gathered the backup company, dragging it to the edge of the forest. This served as an encouragement to my troops that had been kicked out of their trench and managed to retake it, not twice, but three times. Enemy fire made a massacre of my boys, whose lines were getting thinner and thinner. Lieutenant Rabajoli, wounded, struggled to keep the position with his platoon. Lieutenant Galluzzo, gravely wounded in one leg, remained among his Alpini, and could not do anything but beckon them to resist. Three, four, five times my Arditi had to retreat, abandoning their trench. They assaulted it repeatedly, conquering it with admirable courage and tenacity. Yet, the casualties only went up. Around us there was nothing but dead and wounded. My ensigns begged me for reinforcements and ammunition. We did not have any news from those two companies pushed to attack the flanks. The backup company from the Eighty-Fourth Infantry stayed lining the woods. No news of reinforcements from the valley! What was to be done? We did not want to lose our advantage or our position!

Lieutenant Umberto Umerini

It was in that moment that Lieutenant Umerini asked me for men and ammunition. I answered him, asking how many men he had left. "Five," he said. "Then go on the assault with them!" The good Umerini did not whisper, but took off his glasses and cried, "Avanti Savoia!" Running up the blood-covered slope, he pulled along those five Arditi, the same who had been forced to retreat for a sixth time. He once again led with his courageous example. Arriving a few meters from the trench, that valiant officer was hit by a bullet right in his forehead and fell into the arms of his soldiers. What to do now? I had almost no ammunition left. The officers were all either dead or wounded. I had only about fifty Arditi left. With my heart broken, I clenched my fists in rage. I put myself at the head of the backup company and tried to push those soldiers into the trench. It was a vain effort. Overcoming this final mountain peak, stained crimson red with blood and riddled with bullets, was a difficult, almost inhuman task. A young Lieutenant from the Eighty-Fourth Infantry fell in my arms, a brave and valorous soldier who was wounded in his chest. As he was dying, he left me with kind words to comfort me. Blessed be his soul!

It was then I saw the chef of the Officer's Canteen arriving, a certain Gnocchi. He had been preparing soup for our return when a bomb from a 152mm gun sent the container and its contents flying. He picked up his rifle, relieved to be given an excuse to kill the enemy. He caught up with us on the mountain where he could unleash his anger over being interrupted in his meal preparations.

Who could have counted the acts of valor accomplished that day? They were innumerable. They were all heroes, exhausted and cut down, but they never gave up even when their ammunition and officers were in short supply.

In the second trench, Lieutenant Galluzzo died a most heroic death. I already told of how he was wounded in the leg and never retreated from his trench. His Alpini had to abandon him, and he remained at his post, pretending he was dead. At the sixth taking of the trench, when I ordered them to occupy the above trench, the Alpini charged and reached it, holding it for a little time. The poor Galluzzo wished to follow them and dragged himself, limping, up to the parapet. There he was, grappling its edge with his hands and teeth. As he struggled to get himself up, a cruel Austrian brute picked up a large rock and dropped it on the head of poor Galluzzo. There he remained, a sublime spectacle of heroism and duty, suspended on the trench's parapet that he so dearly wished to conquer.

No medal was given to that modest hero, but his memory is equally surrounded by glory and his name is alive with us. His poor mother can be proud of him.

There also fell valiant Divina, a volunteer from Trentino. He was a noble soul with a heart that knew no fear. He died with Italy's name between his lips!

Hundreds of my Arditi died there. They now populate the realm of heroes, in which the first Arditi Company Baseggio, "heroic preface of Italian arditismo, disbanded in death and remembered in eternity, has an honorable spot."

Some survivors of the company

On April 12th, 1916, the survivors gathered in a field near Scurelle. Before returning to their respective units, Captain Baseggio gave them these parting words:[63]

> Arditi, you have been my loyal companions during eight months of combat and sacrifice to achieve the sacred ideal of a free and independent homeland. In leaving you, I feel the need and the duty to thank you. You, who have made my task easy with your

---

[63] This excerpt is officially documented as the motivation for the silver medal given to Captain Baseggio: "Commander of an isolated column of 1500 men, he attacked two heavily fortified peaks many marching hours away from his main division. In two days of gory fighting, they conquered the first positions and immediately sent for reconnaissance to the second position, which was defended by a battalion. The following day it took over seven times in deadly skirmishes to take the second position. Without any forces left, he gathered the few men remaining and after having them line up in the open he inspected their weapons. He then paraded them at regular pace in front of the enemy who, amazed, ceased firing and abandoned their position, offering space for the successive maneuvers of the division." Saint Osvaldo (Sugana Valley), April 3th–6th, 1916.

enthusiastic, intelligent and ardite work and with your immutable faith in our dangerous work.

This act will show how your captain was always a devoted and sincere friend, even if at times strict. He was almost like a father that felt for you more love than a cursory glance could reveal; almost like a father who now cries for the early death of many of his dear sons. That is what all the fallen were for me on that mountain. For many months it was our dream and desire to conquer it. Now it is the simulacra, the effigy of Death and Glory.

Not everyone, oh Arditi, has appreciated your conduct of sacrifice and devotion towards country, filled with goodness and courage, irradiated by the light of glory that the blood of your brothers has imbued upon you all. Yet, in me and in all those who admired you, modest yet valiant warriors, the memory of your work and the glorious pages you have written in the history books of war will never die. Let this be a comforting thought amidst the bitterness of those who should have, and could have, awarded you for a sacrifice worthy of ancient heroes. You see that I am above these grotesque vanities and so these words have greater weight coming from me, who has seen you fight by my side. I am old and nearing the end of a life full of hard work and combat, yet still brightened by pure ideals. Yet while breath remains in me, I will cherish the memories of those inexpressible days that I spent with you.

Return, oh comrades, to your units and take with you the memory of our dead and the love of your captain. Spread among the new troops that Spirit Ardito, that faith, that impetus and let them know of the combat methods I have taught you. These are the only things that allowed victory to be achieved.

You, the valiant that are left, have delivered to me the glorious banner of our company. When you return to your original units, you return as apostles of my ideas. Maybe some of you will again be soldiers in new and more numerous groups of Arditi.

Trenches and Chapel of Saint Osvaldo

Conclusion

Thus, arditismo was born and popularized itself in our war. Arditismo does not only mean a special combat method, freed from formal and rigid disciplinary schemes, but it especially reflects the faith and the audacity of the soul as it pushes itself to try impossible tasks and to face danger. At its root is the love of country and faith in the commander.

The Italian Army owes a lot to arditismo and its Arditi. Our country owes them for the final victory. It owes them for the fruit of the constant struggle sustained by those magnificent troops during the long months and grueling actions in 1916–1917, during the frightening days of defeat, during the months full of anxiety and inexhaustible fights in the consuming defense of the Piave, until the bright impetuous charge of Vittorio Veneto. There, most of all, daring and superior maneuvers triumphed over numbers and means. The tiresome old method of fighting, that had kept our troops in muddy trenches, has been condemned to fade away. Those Arditi of the Baseggio Company were magnificent even in their apparent disorder in dress. Their actions may have been disjointed at times, yet they were always effective. More than just soldiers dedicated to the discipline of form, they were warriors of substance. They were always animated by an offensive spirit, upheld by that faith and enthusiasm that made it easy to forgive their acts of indiscipline, which were, after all, more superficial than substantial.

I saw renowned Generals, as rigorous and as severe as General Graziani, General Farisoglio, and General Spiller, exalted by the show that those troops were giving them, and for the acclaim of their successes. They all agreed that in a war like ours, it is impossible to discern the right men from among the masses of recruited soldiers. The soldier is forced into a state of mediocre physical and moral quality. It is necessary that the special and elite troops are led by commanders who demonstrate their worth only through circumstance. They cannot prepare themselves in schools. They are free from rigid tactical norms. They must be given plentiful resources and liberty of movement to conquer difficult positions, to act as vanguard for the other troops and inspire them with their example or overcome more easily the first and most terrible moments of the melee.

Arditismo is a faith. It is a noble and elevated sentiment, which in war has created valiant soldiers and in the post-war period, has recalled its scholars to defend the country against internal enemies and all causes for national dissolution.

In the war, the Arditi were among the first to propel us towards victory. In peace, we owe to them the first and hardest attacks against Bolshevism and the rampant red scum in Italy from 1919 to 1929. The Fascists educated themselves in the school of arditismo. The majority of those who championed the cause in the first years of the Fascist Revolution were adherents of arditismo.

Arditismo is, and always will be, a school for young Italians, who learn to fight, to show courage in the face of immense danger, and to prepare for the hardest battles in defense of their country.

It pains me to say that the Arditi have not been sufficiently appreciated by past governments or the population. Worried by their exuberance and turbulent nature, they wished to relegate them to the realm of memory.

Of the Death Company, little has been written up to this point. This silence was possibly because I did not want to appear arrogant.

A mixed platoon of the Company

Given the modern and just struggle to promote the measures for our victory and the national values, we must not forget those first Arditi. They put everything at stake when it was dangerous to be bold and daring. They asked for nothing in return. They were simply proud of their sacrifice and their duty towards their beloved Italy.

Appendix A:
Correspondence from Military Personnel

Telegram sent by His Eminence General Andrea Graziani
(Commander of the Pasubio Sector in 1916)

December 1916

Dear Baseggio,

To my brother in arms. Champion of Italian valor, that with only a fistful of men, tore many Trentine territories from the hated enemy. Stop. To his beloved companion, a flower of gentle virtue. Stop. To the two beautiful souls cast in the pure ideals of country and family, I send vivid auspices of happiness in their most welcome day of marriage. Stop. We fight, win, will fight and will win to give a proper nation to all sons of Dante who are oppressed in foreign lands.

Signed,
General Graziani

Baseggio: This dispatch came to me towards the end of 1916 when I got married, during an interval between actions on the Pasubio and those successive actions on the Carso in 1917. I publish it because it represents not only a recognition of the work done by me, which is already one of my most dearly held prizes, but because it reveals the strong and gentle soul of this great General and fervent patriot. Italy owes its salvation to him. The invasion by the enemy could have been fatal, if not for the fierce resistance by the troops of General Graziani on the Pasubio from August to December 1916.

Letter from His Eminence General Andrea Graziani (Head of Her Majesty's First Army in 1915)

Valgatara (Verona), March 5th, 1922

Dearest Baseggio,

From your last letter transpires a sense of profound bitterness in your soul, which I know to be very lively and restless. It is equally concerning because I saw you engaged in painful controversies and political struggles aiming (this I say crossing myself) to sarcastically downplay, and at times, to disseminate doubts on the reality of the labor you have given for Italy as a volunteer of war in the years 1915–1916.

I fully realize the extent of your state of mind, and I comprehend it entirely. I am also certain that, in your strength of character and firm conscience, you will soon find reasons for serenity and further proof that the triumph of truth lays in time alone.

Direct personal interest and passion can, temporarily, hold even men of a certain unquestionable merit from getting to the bottom of a historical search. Laziness could, for a time, lead individual citizens that make up the masses to unconsciously follow the social currents artificially created and perpetuated.

I can already see the day when truth, bare of all veils, frills, and shades, makes its way alone and clearly presents a crystalline and everlasting history.

I am sure that this will be your fate because facts cannot be destroyed. There are too many witnesses. Many are the men alive today that have seen. They know and they do not forget.

When and how was your Explorers Company born? The "Baseggio Company," like the Fifteenth Division of Fifth Army Staff of First Army called it.

It was sooner said than done.

I clearly remember that after the conquest of Mount Salubio at the end of spring 1916—the action in which you were with an extremely forward platoon—you were given the much-desired mission to create a company of volunteers for ardite operations. That company would go on to be strong (thirteen officers, four hundred fifty men, supply mules and machine guns) and excellently organized to operate independently. You instituted it in just a few weeks, and you immediately trained its aggressive spirit, giving chase to two Austrian companies of the Wolker brothers, owners of Ivano Castle.

The aggressive spirit and solidarity that your company acquired in such a short time had been well understood when, with a true warrior's soul, you went looking for the enemy in the mountains. Marching many hours away from the lines of the Fifteenth Division, and with three fierce skirmishes where much blood was spilled, fortune smiled upon your tenacity. You conquered the three forward positions of the Glockenthurm, Mount Collo and Saint Osvaldo.

Those actions gave us much-needed breathing room on the main front for the division (then deployed on the Borgo/Mount Salubio/Mount Armentera Line) and contributed greatly to boosting the morale of all our soldiers in that particularly important sector, while lowering the morale of the enemy.

The inherent importance of the Saint Osvaldo and Mount Collo positions can best be explained by the actions of the Alpini Battalions, who in March had expanded and defended the heights of Saint Osvaldo. I also had the good fortune of seeing the repeated attacks of the Austrian "Strafe Expedition" fail on Mount Collo against the battalions of the Jonio Brigade.

I say to you again, it is useless to invoke past facts which are already well known, at least to the troops of the Fifteenth Division that operated in the Sugana Valley at that time.

In examining your actions as Commander of the Volunteer Arditi Company, I maintain that your work is one of the first of its kind. I do not doubt that your work will be deservedly loved and appreciated as time goes on. It will be an appreciation that will recompense you for the love you bear your company.

Remind the lady of me and be kind in giving her a good handshake from me.

From your old friend,
F. To General Andrea Graziani

Letter from Lieutenant General Farisoglio
(Commander of the Fifteenth Infantry Division)

Merate (Como), March 20th, 1923

Dear Baseggio,

Now that I am in the Special Auxiliary position for the reduction of organics, I spend much of my time with my memories. Naturally, my thoughts prefer to linger on the sweet memories and not the painful ones. Among those that I keep with much delight are the actions of the first Explorers Arditi Company of the Fifteenth Sugana Valley Division, a company constituted, conceptualized, and well commanded with your fortuitous intuition.

There was not even a symptom of any similar intuition from any other division. The need to have men on hand capable of ardimento, who could throw their hearts into the enemy trenches and be fully confident in their abilities to get them back intact, was felt by everyone.

When we later read in the official communications the praises for the splendid actions carried out by you and your men all along the front of the First Army, we thought, "Eh! They have to believe it now!" as Pascarella said. It seemed most appropriate.

This also meant that we had won our bet and as soon as the other commands were capable of doing it, they imitated us with the institution of the Arditi Battalions. These were justified and brought to the height of recognition, but few had in their combat records such heroic actions as the exploration and attack of the Carbonile, or the occupations of Mount Collo, Colle San Giovanni and Mount Saint Osvaldo. It was in these places that your company performed miracles and sacrificed the best of its blood.

In my opinion, any time your lordship would go out with his company for an act of war, it always returned deserving of a medal of valor. At that time, unfortunately, they were distributed too sparingly.

It should please you that today, and always, you will have the pride of having opened the eyes of those in the Superior Command of the necessity of the Arditi departments who, like our Explorers Company, would flush out the enemy and bring back a sure victory.

A good handshake from your ancient Commander of the Fifteenth Division.

F. To Lieutenant General Farisoglio

Letter from His Excellence General Clerici
(First Petty Officer of Her Majesty in the First Army)

Rome, February 23rd, 1922

Dear Baseggio,

I have no doubts that you have constituted the first autonomous Arditi Company, which was born, in fact, in 1915 from the Sugana Valley.

With it you were always on the front line and participated in the operations of Mount Collo with Graziani. I think that not even then among the Germans was there talk of "Assault Troops," and it had most certainly not been talked about among our ranks either.

Cordial Greetings.

F. To Aff.^{MO} your friend,

Clerici

Letter from His Excellence General Roberto Brusati
(Commander of the First Army)

Milan, March 1st, 1922

Esteemed Captain,

I remember that the command of the army, in the period which pertained to me, had much to praise on various occasions of your excellent and efficient ardite work.

To corroborate my memories after almost five years, and to answer your letter with more detail and accuracy, I thought about asking General Clerici, my junior officer of Major Staff for the duration of my command in the First Army. He answered me using these precise phrases:

It is true that Captain Baseggio was tasked on the brink of 1915 to create an Explorers Company that operated in the Sugana Valley sector. With the company, Captain Baseggio distinguished himself many times, especially in the operations of Mount Saint Osvaldo and Mount Collo, in which he brilliantly collaborated with General Graziani, who was then commander of the brigade.

I am incredibly happy that the words of General Clerici fundamentally confirm the correctness of my memories with regards to your good conduct in war. I think that General Farisoglio would have similar things to say, as he was Division Commander at that time, or General Negri, who succeeded him when General Graziani headed the brigade.

I give you my best greetings and wishes for your conduct in war to be appreciated by everyone as it truly deserves.

F.To Aff.^{MO} yours,
Roberto Brusati

Letter from General Spiller
(Head of Her Majesty's Fifteenth Infantry Division 1915–1916)

Naples, March 24th, 1922

Dear Baseggio,

It is true that, officially, you have not been recognized as the founder of the Arditi Staff, but only because they were officially instituted later with an actual rank. Even before their official establishment, however, corps and departments with men of great spirit and body, special traits, and with an aptitude for special missions were constituted, due to the increased pressure to create such units.

You were made the head of these squads many times for reconnaissance and coup de mains, during the period that I was part of the Fifteenth Division. During that time, we brought our occupation further along the ancient border of the Fassa Alps to Mount Salubio, Borgo and Mount Armentera.

Although I am no longer in the Fifteenth Division, I came to know that in the last months of 1915 you were tasked with the formation and leading of a stronger department, a company of Arditi, I believe, with which you operated in the Sugana Valley. In 1917, the regular assault departments were created. In the same year, you were called by me to take part in the command of the Thirteenth Army Staff and to ensure the success of the operations against the Austrians. We studied landing operations with special assault troops, with volunteer elements taken from every unit of the Third Army. You were specially tasked with the organization of this group because I knew about what you had done in the Sugana Valley.

As is often the case, the assault departments did not spring up all at once. They gathered and perfected themselves little by little through forces caused by the necessities of war, until they were officially regulated and organized.

I do not know if any commands before the Fifteenth Division created special departments, with special individuals, for special missions. I do not believe so. Certainly, we must trace the origin of the assault departments to those first corps lead by you in the first months of war, and to the departments later created in October.

Even if you have not been given the official honor of being its creator, I believe it is a thing of pure form which does not alter the substance.

Aside from anything else, only one institution could create the new army staff: The Supreme Command.

At any rate, my dear Baseggio, people like me know you and know what you have done and how much you are worth. Let the ones who doubt your valor bring forward their facts and testimonies. I confirm that they are incapable of doing so.

I saw you work in the Sugana Valley and the Carso, and I took full advantage of your forces, pushing them to their very limits.

With affection,
F.To General Spiller

Letter from Lieutenant Orazio Pedrazzi

Jerusalem, September 12th, 1927

Sir Major,

Regarding the acts of Saint Osvaldo, I was merely a spectator, not a participant. As such, I do not speak for myself when I remember that the first, the very first Italian Arditi caught themselves a furious battle on that glorious day, which showed all the measure of their skills and spirit of sacrifice. The fate of those who fell and the epic calm of those who remained renders certain scenes of somberness and respect for the fallen amongst unrelenting death. They are not acts done in war, but in epics; history will have to remember them. After eleven years, the first Arditi are finally remembered. Italians will never forget them again.

To you, Sir Major, who appeared to us in the Sugana Valley as an adventurous captain, almost a miracle worker, to you who carried the troops like a gust of victorious wind through the enemy lines, all the Sugana Valley will bless you. The dead of Saint Osvaldo, to which you gave the honors of war in front of the Austrian horde, certainly blesses you from the heavens.

Orazio Pedrazzi

Letter from Lieutenant Colonel Mazzuchelli
(Officer in the Command Staff of the Fifteenth Division)

Florence, March 9th, 1922

Dear Baseggio,

I do not know how it is possible to cast doubt upon what you have said. It must come from persons who have not had the pleasure of meeting you during that period of action of the Fifteenth Infantry Division in the Sugana Valley in the first year of the war.

I, who has lived with you through those hours of trepidation and impetus, can affirm with whole conscience, that you were the first to constitute a mixed company from various departments. The Explorers Company Arditi Baseggio was what you called it in 1915, during your stay in Ivano Castle with the Command Staff of the Fifteenth Division.

To your company were always reserved the most audacious actions, the most dangerous ones, the most desperate of attacks, on Mount Collo, on Mount Saint Osvaldo, etc.

It is perfectly correct to assert that you thought up, constituted, and led this same department for over seven months and before any similar ones had been constituted.

I remember very well how His Excellency General Sailer had entrusted you with the constitution of the Arditi Battalion of the Third Army, and that together, with another battalion of Arditi cyclists, would have executed the landing on Nabresina.

The medals of valor that you have earned, and the relationships that you must still hold with the great commanders of your war operations, are proof enough.

In Kindness,
F.To Lieutenant Colonel Mazzuchelli

Letter from Medic Captain B. Signorelli

Tarvisio, February 16th, 1923

Dear Baseggio,

I have read, with rightful pride, the pages of *The Death Company*. It is your apologia, as well as that of your men.

I do not want to judge the treatment given to you by the superior authorities.

Let the love and eternal memory that the survivors of the glorious company hold for you be of comfort. They, who on a night in April 1916, on Telve di Sopra, acclaimed you as a victor worthy of the highest reward for valor. At the same time, in a car in the square, the stern and cold face of General Graziani was covered by heartfelt tears.

I remember that after you disbanded the company on Saint Osvaldo, the Command Staff in Ivano Castle wanted to give us a new, trusted commander to take your place. In the name of all your Arditi, I went to the Aide-de-Camp for General Amari to notify him that no captain in the army was worthy of holding a spot held by you.

As another token of gratitude for your high valor, the company was officially disbanded the following day!

I remember that after the action on the Glockenthurm, you proposed to give some of us medals for valor that evening in the canteen. We decided to refuse them if a silver medal for valor was not given to you, as we were convinced that on that day you were the most valiant among the valiant, the most Ardito among the Arditi. Another recognition and reward for your valor!

I would not stop writing if I wanted to recall the entire epic of those eight months in the Death Company. The highest reward for us survivors is being able to rejoice in having been part of your company; to have served our country with great sacrifice and loyalty that now pushes our consciences calmly towards the honor and grandeur of Italy, to which we still offer up our weapons, ready for your call and command.

With warm regards,
B. Signorelli

Letter from General Spiller

Milan, September 19th, 1927

Painfully, I am not able to attend the ceremony for reasons of service. I thank the committee for the kind invitation. With a touched spirit, I join the honoring feast for the Baseggio Company, precursor to the Arditi departments. From its leader to its last gregarious member, it gave proof on the field of supreme patriotic love and disregard for life, giving numerous casualties to measure their valor.

General Spiller

Salluzzo, March 5th, 1925

The officers of the Second Group, First Mountain Artillery Regiment that have admired the actions of the Volunteer Company Baseggio in the Sugana Valley in 1915–1916, extend their expression of vivid pleasure because of the recognition of the high valor of its commander, Cristoforo Baseggio.

Como, September 9th, 1927

To the Pro Ricordo Caduti Saint Osvaldo Committee, Roncengo,

I have received the courteous invite that has been sent to me for the ceremony that will occur on the eleventh day, to commemorate the glorious fallen of the Arditi Company Baseggio in Roncengo. Sadly, I cannot attend. I send, through this envoy, a devoted thought for the heroic fallen and respect for the eternal remembrance given to them.

Arturo Cittadini
General of the Army Corps

Turin, September 10th, 1927

Remembering the heroic work of the Sugana Valley Arditi, I painfully regret that I must be absent. Yet, I take lively part in the solemn ceremony in spirit, and I send respectful regards to you, Valorous Leader of the Undefeated Maniple.

General Clerici

Certosa (Bolzano), September 8th, 1927

Honorable Committee,

Sadly, I cannot attend your ceremony in honor of the heroes fallen on Saint Osvaldo and of its valorous commander, Major Baseggio, who has kindly invited me. I am still high in the mountains with my battalion, and I cannot come down. I beg of you to make my presence known in spirit for this patriotic ceremony, which I acknowledge with all my heart. Glory to the pioneers of Italian arditismo! Blessed be the fallen of Saint Osvaldo.

With the utmost respect,
Lieutenant Colonel M. De Castiglione

Rome, September 10th, 1927

As I am immobilized here in Rome, I send to the heroic precursor of the Arditi and the valiant survivors of Saint Osvaldo, along with the desperate sublime fallen of the Baseggio Company, my brotherly and respected salute of black flame that has made heroism its highest religion.

ALALÀ![64]

Mario Carli

---

[64] [Ancient Greek, meaning "battle-cry" or "war-cry." Alala was the female personification of the war cry in Greek mythology. This war-cry was used by the Arditi during World War I and was adopted by the Fascist movement.]

Frescorre, September 11th, 1927

To your fallen firstborn of Italian arditismo I give my reverent salute, and to you, heroic animated commander, a brother's hug.

Giannino Antona Traversi

Rome, September 10th, 1927

We few, who lived the revolt and redemption of the masculine in 1919 for the salvation of country and nation, rally around the arditismo of the Death Company. On Saint Osvaldo, they received a crown of oak and laurel. The short roman sword shines. It is rooted in every ardite battle that has the name Justice in its heart and the always firm thought in the frontier against an unchanging enemy.

Bolzon

Milan, September 10th, 1927

I join with warm admiration the glorious tribute of gratitude rendered upon these heroic comrades, Ardite Explorers Baseggio.

Gervasoni

S. Candicci, September 10th, 1927

As I cannot attend, I send to the heroic Major Baseggio, conqueror of Saint Osvaldo, an enthusiastic brotherly salute, kneeling before the valiant fallen.

Colonel Mazzuchelli

Civitavecchia, September 10th, 1927

On this solemn day, I send to you devoted thoughts for the heroic fallen. I salute the survivors and applaud Major Baseggio for his marvelous undertaking.

Lieutenant Colonel Zani

Captain Zani
Fifteenth Division Commander

Appendix B:
Newspaper Articles

From the Gazzetta del Popolo in Turin
(Article by Orazio Pedrazzi, August 1916)

The Death Company

It seemed like the Garibaldine spirit would find its end with the advent of modern warfare. It seemed that the machine would have overpowered man, reducing him to a tool for war like a rifle or a bayonet. It was said that courage was no longer necessary, that only discipline mattered. Yet, all that *is* necessary is courage. Courage and obedience. The influence of German ideas has torn from our souls even the beautiful faith in our instinctive racial resources, putting stifling and annoying regulations in place of our wonderful Italian nerves and resolve.

Therefore, at the outbreak of war, it was understood that war should have been regulated, even in its most miniscule movements. It was not a just gigantic show of human action, a superb act of force utilized only to achieve victory. It referred also to the tenacious will of heroic individuals.

Trench warfare was said to be resistance more than ardor, tenacity without impetus. The ardite exploits of the Garibaldine troops at Argonne are brought up to demonstrate how their sublime heroism only served to massacre them. Finally, it was said that "for these so-called heroes, only the sky and the depths of the sea are left." They had forgotten the mountains, which was inexcusable in Italy. They had forgotten that on the plains of western France and eastern Prussia the terrain imposed flat and monotonous warfare. Heroism changed its form into a terrible physiognomy, strained by resistance until putrefaction occurred in those humid underground trenches. In Italy, the grand mountain ranges, the ruinous valleys, the eternal snowing, and horrendous ravines give to war a character which denotes the predominance of man over machine, of force and personal courage over rigid methodology and unflinching regulations.

Mount Saint Osvaldo

The difficulty and natural danger of the mountains is so tremendous that none of the proud soldiers fighting in the plains could have even imagined it. Most of the world ignores them. Even warfare in mountains is something else entirely, infinitely harder than war on the plains, but also infinitely more picturesque. Maneuvering in mountains is just like the old wars grandfathers tell us about, where fighting takes on an ancient and glorious appearance. It is made up of assaults, climbs, ambushes, and incredible demonstrations of arditismo that could have been taken directly from the poems of Ariosto or Tasso.[65] In those days, men scaled the battlements of castles; now we scale the peaks of unreachable mountains. They crossed ditches and moats around well-defended walls; now we jump over crevasses and ravines and cut through forests to reach these natural "fortresses" of the enemy.

It is the Garibaldine Spirit that takes its revenge and surges back up. In the soul of that old race, it rushes with great leaps, jumps like flashes of lightning, and makes sparks of all that is irregular. It has all the strength and all the weaknesses of genius.

The Alps, that before had seen the Garibaldine militias advance and win until the *Obbedisco*.[66] The Alps, who before had seen the feats of the irregulars of *Cadore*.[67] In this war that was destined to be of German brand and style, this war that was supposed to be of automatons, those mountains see those beautiful ranks of volunteers, those poor devils, the units of neck-breaking souls, willing to die rather than stand idle. The Alps see those who would defiantly hold the banner of the futurist motto: "*Marciare non Marcire!*"[68]

In those valleys and up those mountains, passed the winds of war like in the times of the Orlando.[69] The Death Company made sure of it.

---

[65] Ludovico Ariosto (1474–1533) was an Italian poet best known for the romance epic *Orlando Furioso* ["The Frenzy of Orlando" or "Raging Roland"]. Torquato Tasso (1544–1595) was also an Italian poet best known for his poem *Gerusalemme liberate* [Jerusalem Delivered].

[66] Reference to the famous telegram Garibaldi sent to General Alfonso La Marmora that only contained the word, *Obbedisco* ("I Obey"). Garibaldi was advancing with unstoppable force into the Austrian lines during the Third Italian War of Independence when he was ordered to stop.

[67] Troops from the Alpine Brigade "Cadore," a light infantry brigade of the Italian Army. The brigade was mostly made up of Alpini units.

[68] ["Run, do not rot!"]

[69] Reference to the "Orlando Furioso" ["The Frenzy of Orlando" or "Raging Roland"],

The Leader and His Workers

Out of a Garibaldine reflex, the command of the division instituted the new department, destined to participate in exploration and the most desperate and ardite feats.

The proclamation asked its dependent troops from every corps and corner of the army to volunteer. Volunteers were offered both danger and glory.

> You will be the first. Any action where death or glory are required will be for you. You will not have the typical military life. You will not be exempt from fatiguing services. All sacrifices will be asked of you in battle. We shall give you a fitting leader.

Ah, their leader!

The leader was a sacred and worthy position in the Death Company. The soldiers who left their posts to rendezvous with death did not ask who their officer would be, but who their *leader* would be.

The company assumed a personal character and took its courage from the authority and impetus of their commander. The character of these Alpini groups was recognized even by the Supreme Command, who christened them with the very name of their commander. We can all imagine what decisive influence the leader had on the actions of the Death Company. What a wonderful, adventurous soldier was he who commanded it!

A look at his face was all that was needed to tell he was a man of steel with unbreakable nerves, hard like granite in his propositions and thoughts. He was everything but a common man. He could register acute dislike, but also boundless admiration. He was excluded from remaining indifferent.

Dressed casually in his alpine uniform, yet with an imposing air, he had in his implacable eyes the fire and tenacity of an exceptional fighter.

---

an Italian epic poem written by Ludovico Ariosto. It is the pinnacle of chivalric romance and includes various genres. It tells of the adventures of Roland, a paladin fighting against the Saracen invasion of Europe.

His life was like that of the medieval wandering knights that sought out something to quench their insatiable restlessness and sense of adventure. He was an Alpine Officer, among the first of his class at the school of war. He was deployed in a myriad of operations from Africa to America. He adapted to the primitive life of virgin nations and the refined civility of decadent nations alike. He was always battling and fighting with one thing or another. Throughout his adventurous career, he hardened his physical exterior and his emotional well-being like the old plants in the tropical climates hardened their outer shells. The result was a fearless man—maybe good, maybe evil—but undoubtedly an exceptional soldier, a marvelous captain of men.

Those who joined had to be like this as well, those desperate men needing to put their warrior's skills to the test in some dangerous maneuver. The same could be said for the captains of the American wars, the captains of pirate ships, or the adventurers that emerged from South Africa and the golden basin regions.

Around the captain, tried and true with the deep scars of an intense life, stood a motley group of dreamers and those seeking glory. From various regiments came seasoned officers who enthusiastically joined the Death Company. These were men who disdained long periods of inactivity and unnerving slowdowns, who longed to fight, fight, fight! There were young eighteen-year-olds, with eyes still full of naivety and poetry, and junior lieutenants fresh from school, still dreaming of their first loves. These were men who, at one of the most profound times in history, asked that their solemn lives bestow to them the greatest emotions and the most rage-filled visions, eager to trade them with death.

That gang of turbulent officers and soldiers, who beat their chests and sang with all the good and bad exuberances of their goliardic temperament, constituted an oasis of youth more vigorous than ever. A life stronger than before. Those ranks of young upstarts sometimes upset nearby units, but eventually won them over in the end, earning their profound admiration. They acted like a horde of warrior poets, stoking the flames of our enthusiasm, and pushing us further up to where the souls of heroes are set free.

Their uncontrollable ardor was so contagious that even the medic of the company, an elderly, silver-haired gentlemen, acted as if he was twenty and competed with the younger ones in all their merry and heroic feats.

The soldiers resembled their officers in every way. There was nothing more picturesque than that mosaic-like department in which the long and proud feathers of the Alpini mingled with the large, plumed hats of the Bersaglieri, with the yellow insignia of the Finanzieri, and with the uniforms of artillerymen and infantrymen. When they were deployed, they looked like a hastily assembled, rag-tag mixture of the entire army. Giving a closer look to them individually, they all looked a bit shabby. Yet together they formed a superbly colorful tangle of uniforms under which beat true warrior hearts.

Indeed, they were not all well-disciplined. There were those who had come to the company simply to put the Explorer's Star on their arms. Some wished to be the first in every assault. Some could bear the strict commands and everyday discipline. Some sought more liberty in exchange for having to face danger more often.

It was often the case that soldiers with disciplinary reprimands asked to be sent among the Arditi. If they had the guts and will to fight hard, they were welcomed with open arms into the company, despite their past sins.

In fact, what would the Death Company have done with soldiers who were a little too docile and placid? Let them be cunning smugglers, or even anarchists, so long as they were always valorous. That was the fundamental idea behind recruitment in that exceptional department. It took in the most troublesome soldiers from other units and guided them with an iron fist in every assault. Most Austrians they fought were terrified, fleeing before them with their tails tucked between their legs.

Many smugglers who offered the Alpini their knowledge of the insidious mountains and their many footpaths were taken into the company with a renewed sense of national brotherhood. They did not regret standing side by side with their enemies of yesterday, the Finanzieri, sometimes even finding comfort in their company.

What did it matter what had happened in their pasts? Their new lives, inebriated by joy and danger, brought together these soldiers with diverse backgrounds and different military exploits. They were all united in their faith for their captain and ready, at his every word, to gladly sacrifice their very lives for their brothers and their beloved Italy.

The Feats

The company had to "hammer" the enemy. The men threw themselves into the fray wherever they were most needed, surprising, and mauling the adversary to unnerve him. They moved quickly during their exploring maneuvers, acting as the fast and impetuous arm of the division.

It can be said that if these ranks of valiant break-necks had been at the disposal of an entire army, rather than just a single division, their actions would have filled many more pages in the history of war in the valleys of the Trentino.

Yet, in the small divisional environment, the Death Company found its stops and respites in various villages constantly interrupted by skirmishes that turned into fast and intense victories. The snowy peaks of the Montalon, already a witness of failed invasions by our army in days of frozen hails, had given the company their baptism by fire and ambitious praises by Superior Command. At Forcella Magna, the mountains slammed the explorers with avalanches, pushing them into harsh fights against the snow and ice. Soldiers who were swept away worked hard to free themselves, and to reestablish interrupted communication lines. Yet because of the languid situation of the army's front, the company was also forced into unexpected periods of forced rest, until again it had to leave its trenches for a raid. Those raids would remain among the most significant in mountain warfare.

Our forces were still in the old lines of Borgo that cut the Sugana Valley. They ran on one side along the ridges of the Armentra and on the other along the Pasubio and Cista. The enemy was in front from Roncengo and beyond. All the mountain slopes that climbed towards Mount Saint Osvaldo, the Glockenthurm, Fravort and Mount Collo were occupied by the Austrians, who had a safe shelter for their patrols and huts spread along the forests and mule tracks.

The Death Company volunteered to burn those huts and an attack was launched.

It was necessary to leave our lines spread along the mountains, scout the enemy terrain and find the enemy positions. They marched more than ten kilometers from their trenches in terrain ravaged by enemy artillery shelling, with no link to the rest of the troops, to find the enemy.

It was truly an action of guerilla tactics and downright banditry. The innate valor of the Explorers, their desire for dangerous adventures, and their unshakeable positivity found ample space for a magnificent result. The attack was a success.

They had left in the morning, climbing through snow, sleeping on ice for two days, eating burnt chestnuts and cooked apples, and skirting between enemy patrols with incredible nonchalance. At night, from our trenches in Borgo, we saw the Austrian positions on the mountain slopes become a bright constellation of fires. The high flames went up along the mount, sparked by the valor of our volunteers. That night, twenty-seven huts stopped housing reinforcements for the enemy. How those Explorers managed to light all those fires is still not precisely known. There was a farmer who had been requisitioned as a guide, and he could probably tell of how this brave feat was accomplished. He was released more dead than alive from fright after that victorious evening.

After a stop at the Saint Brigida Church (or really at the canteen of the saint), the company returned to Borgo that evening. Every soldier had with them war memorabilia gathered from their risky venture. An Austrian flag was the fanciest trophy. The crowd in town applauded the victorious troops, who, after their herculean task, returned drinking and singing to the Italian ranks. Many a man awoke the next day with a hangover from the revelry!

The feats continued to multiply until that tormented month of May, when the vehement Austrian offensive was stopped.

One day the company left to search for the enemy on the Glockenthurm. In the thick fog they arrived at the enemy lines without even realizing it. Although surrounded on three sides, the company managed to escape.

On another day, they crossed Roncegno where enemy patrols still roamed the entire area of Marter, Torrefonda and Fonderia. The first group from Tesoppo knew of the audacity, the courageous imprudence, the intemperance of those volunteers. They knew all the enemy spotters' positions by heart (along with the taste of wine from every cottage along the countryside). They made miracles happen for a single glass of wine! It was not rare among the Explorers to risk their lives in night attacks, moving stealthily under the eyes of the Austrian spotters to reach the houses where the enemy was entrenched, defeat them, and then drink all the wine.

These were the mocking actions of the volunteers, who played a spinet in the trenches and sang songs like "Vedova Allegra," enraging the Austrians in the forward posts. These men sometimes attached strange vegetation to their uniforms or wore clothing found here and there in the villages, bringing contempt from our soldiers. It also infuriated the enemy. The enemy could only look on as he was being provoked by these mischievous soldiers in the opposite trenches.

The tragic day at Saint Osvaldo came in early April. Ever since the foundation of the company, officers and soldiers alike waited for the right occasion to glorify their department with an important success. The skirmishes were all well and good; they all liked the exuberant and bizarre triumphs of the skirmishes, but the volunteers felt the need to engage in more decisive successes and in greater feats.

So, when the order to occupy Saint Osvaldo came, the entire company understood that the time had come for death and glory.

Saint Osvaldo, a sinister and steep mountain, was held by the Austrians like a formidable bulwark against the Sugana Valley. That damned mountain was used by the furious Austrian artilleries to ravage Roncegno and Borgo. Its only match appeared to be the strongest of forces supported by heavy artillery. The company was given the honorable task to take it.

Death was easier than victory. Yet was it not the terrible Goddess Death which the company named itself lovingly after? They embarked on their journey as if it was a great, youthful dance. The officers joked with the troops about the impending action. They left with a firm resolve to reach the little white chapel placed at the top of the coveted mountain, to rip it away from the enemy's clutches and to loudly proclaim their victory from atop the summit.

Damned Saint Osvaldo! From that day, it became the most hated mountain in all the Sugana Valley. Less than three hundred were the assailants. In the trenches and fortified battlements, the enemy awaited them. From on high, one could see that the battle for the lower level of the peak raged on for the entire day. As more and more volunteers died, the ardor and tenacity of those remaining increased and lead them forward in the assault. The machine guns, those cold and unstoppable assassins, did not leave anyone standing; every step taken was a fight.

Yet, seven times they pushed forward, yearning for that white chapel at the top. Torn down by the cannons and shredded by bullets, they finally reached the contested peak and loudly proclaimed their victory!

But how many were left? Half had died along the way. The officers were all either dead or wounded. Lieutenant Galante lay dead, filled with melancholy and sweet southern idealism. Dead was the youngster, Galluzzo, who looked like a child, even when crushed by a boulder pushed down the mountain by the enemy. Dead was the brave Umerini, the Republican journalist who had rushed into the assault with a reserve cut down to just four men. He had fallen heroically at the head of those four. The others were wounded and bleeding, with only their heads untouched by some miracle.

Unfortunately, they had to give up their hard-won position and climb back down the mountain. Their numbers had been too greatly reduced, and they could not resist a counterattack in such an isolated spot.

For the entire day, the sides of that tragic mountain resounded with rifle fire, with screams and curses. The small acts of resistance made by those soldiers who did not want to retreat lasted late into the evening.

When they made a head count, they realized not even a quarter of the company was left alive. So, it was that Saint Osvaldo cruelly delivered bitter death to the Death Company.

The Reward

The company returned to their trenches, carrying the dead bodies of their officers. It was then that the company was dissolved.

Many other units were created later, though none as distinguished as the Death Company. As the Austrian offensive approached, no one thought about refitting that original department, now left with just a few living heroes.

Each one of them returned to their regiment, carrying with them the tragic and fascinating memory of their beloved company.

No officer received a reward. Maybe there was no time to think about these things, or maybe too many were deserving of a medal.

The Arditi left just as they had arrived, as Garibaldi would have, giving up everything and getting nothing in return.

Near the kind village where they were billeted, in the flowery cemetery, there are some tombs lying next to one another. These hold the sacred bodies of those officers who fell in the Mount Saint Osvaldo assault. No one cuts the grass there anymore, after the exodus of the population. The overgrowth covers the little mounds of these heroes with greenery and flowers.

Upon the mountain, in those graves with no names, where the bodies of our men were thrown by the Austrians, lay dozens of volunteers who wanted to win; and to win, they had to die.

Those tombs, those graves, they are the medals of valor for the Death Company.

                                                    Orazio Pedrazzi

Article by Dr. Vacchetta, April 1916

As a friend and often participant in the numerous reconnaissance operations of war which forged this special company, I have been given the task of describing the final, most dangerous, and bloody battle in which that corps of brave men fought and the fame that their actions acquired. The echoes of the Sugana Valley will resound for all time. The company displayed valor in the highest sense of the word. The uncommon arditismo pushed them to enter ranks devoted to sacrifice. It united them in the oaths of loyalty they swore to uphold their duty and their great love of country.

Among those officers and infantrymen, I counted my dearest friends. Now, it is a duty as painful as it is sacred for me, with the insisting wishes of their family and friends, to recount the glorious end of those martyrs.

My poor words will certainly not further their glory, neither will they give more fame to the well deserving survivors. This humble and just homage to the memory of those valiant men will serve as a remembrance and give testament to all about how, in Italy, we know how to give our lives to a higher ideal.

The Explorers Company Arditi Baseggio was greeted by the usual distrust for all things new. I followed it from its first maneuvers and reconnaissance missions, a little driven by my naturally adventurous spirit and a little attracted by the certain charm which that maniple of intrepid men had to all gallant and generous spirits. An old-fashioned officer commanded them. He was still a lieutenant then. Ah, that old lieutenant. That was what the soldiers who had been with him for many months called him, accompanying him on many patrols and scouting missions. He was a man of few harsh words, with hardy lineaments, bright eyes, and a resolute gaze. He rarely spoke, and when he did speak, it was always incisive phrases like the cut of a surgeon's blade. I liked him and followed him many times on his raids. I also liked his officers in much the same way. They exuded life and enthusiasm, and although fearful of their Commander, they were bound to him by a certain love which, as the days passed, cemented their reciprocal trust and respect.

During dark and anxious nights, in the whistling of machine guns and the bursting of bullets, I recognized in those men the best of friends. Soldiers were as lively when billeted as they were marvelous in combat. Life for them was nothing without their commander. Any order given by him would be the most sacred word in existence for them. They watched their comrades from other regiments with pride of course, but with swaggering smiles they called themselves and made themselves to be called "Baseggio Explorers."

For them, there was no other captain or lieutenant, only one Baseggio. There may have been other good officers like Signorelli, Galante, Umerini, and Gagliotti. Yet just like it was for the Red Shirts and Garibaldi, so it was for the Arditi and their Baseggio. A relationship of trust and love came to be between the captain and his gregarious troops. It was cultivated in those long nights of common stress and dangerous situations they had endured together for many long months.

In early April, they left on a night maneuver to try to occupy the peak of Saint Osvaldo. It was an action of great arditismo, and significant sacrifice. Victory was far from certain. The marble chapel, like the eye of Cyclops from high atop the mountain, watched over the Sugana Valley vigilantly, with a defiant and menacing look. It was their dream to reach it. They greatly desired to climb up there, to touch it, to possess it. They stared up, with bleak expressions, as would ancient Knights watching a beautiful maiden who was shackled and protected by a dragon.

Those silent, frenzied ranks marched out, with the feeling of sacrifice already in their hearts, as if heading towards a sacred spring day of blood and honor, from which a greater life flows for the glory and the greatness of Italy.

On Saint Osvaldo they fell. Out of three hundred soldiers, one hundred ninety paid for their ardimento with their blood and their lives. Out of six officers, not one survived. Only the captain was untouched, with the spectacle of death before him, gripping his heart dearly.

The first to fall was Lieutenant Galante, who was shot in the heart while he tried to act as a shield for his commander. The wounded Lieutenant Gagliotti, conqueror of the first trench, enveloped by an enemy four times the size of his maniple, surrounded by dead and dying, encouraged the survivors to not give up. A wounded Lieutenant Medic Signorelli did not abandon his post and kept gathering and attending to the numerous wounded.

The machine guns were sowing death. Behind every tree was an ambush. Every step brought us closer to death. Our sacred ranks were cut down, even while still climbing ever faithfully up that dangerous mountain to save the lives of others. The slopes were harsh. The enemy hardened its defenses and even threw boulders at us! Young Lieutenant Galluzza was assaulting the highest trench. Even while wounded, he insisted on proceeding further. He was killed by a massive rock from above that crushed his skull. Many others had their hands cut off by enemy bayonets while they tried repeatedly to climb the parapets. Lieutenant Umerini, the young Milanese journalist, and a volunteer of war, who had been spared in the Balkans and the Argonne by the enemy and had been wounded at Carso, was writing in that critical moment to his captain. "I have no more than five men at my disposal," he said out loud, as he wrote hurriedly. "Attack with them," his captain answered, having approached Umerini's position in that very same moment. A drop of blood hit the page, the decisive final dot for that phrase in his notebook. He moved his men forward. After only a few steps, a bullet struck his forehead.

Rabajoli, a young officer from Turin, wounded by a grenade and presumed dead, was the first to reach the furthest trench and remained

Lieutenant Rabajoli   *Captain Major Turrin*

there for three hours, lying beside his dead and wounded, without ammunition, refusing to disobey the captain's orders. Amidst an intense volley of rifle fire, we saw him come back at last, smiling, with some of his men. He had procured a bandolier of bullets from the enemy.

But who could tell of all the valorous episodes of soldiers and ensigns on that day? Dozens were wounded, yet they continued to return fire. Stretcher-bearers, calm under the hail of bullets, carried out their solemn duty. Comrades were in tears and did not want to abandon the corpses of their killed officers. Turrin, an Alpino wounded by a projectile exploding near his head, blood gushing from his eye socket, and his eye hanging out, wanted to keep fighting and only begrudgingly obeyed the captain's orders to get medical aid. Impiccini, the cook for the officer's canteen, set out after the enemy to "buy more meat" when his pot was destroyed by enemy fire, blaspheming and with musket in hand. He returned covered in blood, but with four rifles.

For three straight hours, between the lead from the artillery, the sinister popping of exploding balls, the harrowing screams of the wounded, the sobs of the dying, that maniple of valorous comrades took, lost, and re-took the first and second trench seven times! Unfortunately, the enemy arrived at the front and flanks. Their reinforcements grew emboldened, while our ranks became thinner and thinner.

With a sunken soul, surrounded by the dead and wounded, the captain ordered the retreat. Wonder overtook the battlefield when everyone saw those fifty-four survivors, under enemy fire, obey their commander's orders to "count as two" like in Piazza d'Armi, without hesitation. They marched out in parade formation, causing the enemy to cease fire to watch them go in utter amazement.

They were not destined to take that long coveted hill. Their blood, reddening the mountain snow, served as a promise and an invitation to the other units, who were more fortunate and managed to climb and conquer the position the following morning.

That crimson blood, mixed with the white snow and the green of the trees, was the third color that Fate willed not to be united with the other two that day, a symbol of our victorious flag.

Lieutenant Vacchetta, April 1916

A Rite of War in Roncegno:
The Tomb for the Fallen of the Death Company
(September 1927)

On Sunday, at Roncegno di Trento, the commemorative tomb for the fallen of the Arditi Baseggio Company was inaugurated. It was embedded in the chapel of Saint Osvaldo, the mountain renowned for being the final battleground for the company. The entire company was almost lost for the conquest of that mountain.

Present at the ceremony were General Graziani, the Vice Prefect of Trento representing the National Government; the Consul of the Forty-First Legion M.V.S.N., Commander Guido Larcher, representing the Combatants Federation of Trento; the honorable Lunelli for the Fascist Federation; and the surviving officers, ensigns, and soldiers of the company. They all spoke to the crowd of the exemplary feats accomplished by the company.

Major Baseggio commemorates the Battle at Saint Osvaldo, 1927

After His Excellence General Graziani, the Vice Prefect of Trento spoke, the Political Secretary of Roncegno, and the Podestà also spoke. Then Major Baseggio gave the following speech:

Eleven years ago, these valleys resounded with the gloomy roar of artillery and these villages were tormented by the horror of massacres, from the smoke of devastating fires, from the cries of the dead and dying. Forty months of stress, terror, hope, treachery, success, and exasperating failures until that final Italian victory placed Italy back in its true place in the world.

You, inhabitants of these valleys, who have witnessed the innumerable battles, have heard the palpitations of a thousand young hearts that here were sacrificed, that here rest in eternal slumber buried among the green of your fields, are now merry and affluent. You have not forgotten the dead, wounded, and mutilated, who, with their blood, have given you peace and liberty. That is more precious than any other necessity for those who love country and comprehend the fine ideals of life and its sentimental beauty.

On this day, in which the survivors of my company are for the first time united among you, let me remind you of the unforgettable work of all those brave men who defended the Italian spirit. They courageously endured blows from an overwhelming enemy, were strong in victory and dignified in defeat, and faced death hundreds of times for your liberation and for the glory of Italy.

With pride I will dwell on the history of my company, the first autonomous Arditi Volunteer Company. From October 1915 to April 1916, they chased the conquest of the positions dominating the Borgo Basin with their own sacrifices.

Oh, surviving comrades, who for many months fought by my side, let me, your commander and brother, say that I am proud to be here today for the welcomed duty of remembering your acts of valor and the noble sacrifice of the glorious Dead.

I do not want to diminish the merits of others, but to make yours shine brighter.

You, who know me well and love me with much affection that was matured during our difficult patrols. In the bitter assaults, you know that I, in exalting your work, do not wish anything more than to fulfill a sacred duty towards you.

Let it be said that here, where the mountains, the valleys, and the local population can be witnesses, that the true history of what was, and will always be, the creation of the Arditi occurred. Only one year after the glorious end of the first autonomous company, subsequent Arditi units were showing their courage and claiming victories. From 1917 to 1918, they had the duty to, on the Carso and the Piave, and in a hundred more battles, to always be at the head of our troops and pull them forward to victory.

From the beginning of the war, our troops achieved excellent results for individual arditismo. Our soldiers, ensigns and officers of all categories demonstrated their individual and collective valor innumerable times. As officers and soldiers of patrols and major departments, they were always ready and willing to distinguish and ultimately sacrifice themselves. The history of our war is full of these actions, and all fronts are marked by thousands upon thousands of tombs of our obscure heroes.

Other than these isolated examples, no one had yet valued the strength and prestige that came from our armies. Focus was on organizing those few efforts of the courageous into special departments and into actions aiming for a tactical goal. It was also to educate those ardite elements into a single school of thought: of audacity in action, of fluency in methods, of strength in deep assaults, and to dare, above all, to "Triumph or Die."

We had to reawaken the Latin spirit, break the Teutonic formalities, win over inertness, overcome the trenches, and throw ourselves into the chasm with a willful heart and tense nerves, a dagger in our teeth and fire in our eyes. It was all a revolution in methodology: of actions, tactics, and moral education that we had to face under the enemy's onslaught. We had to dare the impossible and face death, for glory and victory.

The merits of having provided the first organic unit of Italian arditismo in war, of having adopted ardite fighting methods of attack and nimble maneuvers, of having disregarded, at times, formal discipline in favor of more sound substance; these all belong to the first autonomous Arditi Company Baseggio and to the Alpine Century of the valorous Captain Castiglioni. They were constituted officially by order of the command of the First Army in 1915, one in the Sugana Valley and the other in the Tellina Valley.

Of the Castiglioni Century, it is enough to say they faced numerous trials and ended up destroyed, earning eternal glory for all their slain.

Of my company, I will say a bit more.

I, who in the first months of war had commanded numerous small ardite actions, had persuaded myself that it was necessary to give our troops the example of what was possible, specifically on mountainous terrain. When commanders are well supported by courage, resilience and in the methods of combat utilized by elite troops trained in guerilla tactics, much initiative and valor is achieved.

Speaking of this with General Graziani and General Clerici, who commanded the First Army, along with General Farisoglio and Colonel Spiller of the Fifteenth Division, I convinced them of the usefulness of trying this experiment. Much to their credit, the constitution of the first autonomous Arditi Volunteer Explorers Company was sanctioned. In Strigno, in October, I united around four hundred fifty men. Among them were officers, ensigns and soldiers chosen from all units and corps of the division. I instructed them, not with maneuvers from Piazza d'Armi, but instead with reconnaissance missions and small skirmishes that allowed me to judge my troops in terms of effective firepower capabilities and terrain practicality.

You remember those courageous men from every class, every age, every rank: Alpini Bersaglieri, artillery and infantry men, Finanzieri, militias of engineer corps, medics and even veterinarians. Great was the desire for combat in that heterogeneous and tumultuous ensemble. Enthusiasm and faith united the philosopher and the common worker, the nationalist and the anarchist, the artisan and the merchant, the farmer and the smuggler. Love for country fused these souls into a single entity.

"The Ardite Ideal"

It was said that they were undisciplined, that they fought for love of plundering and violent instinct. Never was more vile slander spoken! All the Arditi of the Death Company were always ready when danger called. They all knew how to fulfill their duties by observing the most rigid discipline. On Montalon, Forcella Magna, Mount Cima, the Glockenthurm, Marter, Mount Collo, and Volto, my Arditi marked each of these battlegrounds with their blood and the dead, until their triumphal march ended in the gory battle on Saint Osvaldo. It was there that almost all my troops were wounded or killed. It was there, those seven times, that those strong conquerors lost and regained, with bayonets, the enemy's trenches. At the last, without any ammunition left, we lost our ground for the last time and had to retreat down the mountain. We did so in proud, marching parade step.

Oh, unforgettable dead! Oh, Umerini, Galanti, Galluzzo, Divina, Vismara! Oh, many more modest comrades, though not less worthy, who now rest tranquil in the cemeteries of Roncegno, Borgo or Strigno in the shadow of some neglected pine. Your sacrifice was not in vain. Your work was not struck down by death. The ardite ideal has made its way onwards. It has continued, thanks to you, and has been spread by its survivors in all corps from Stelvio to Isonzo. It has vanquished all resistance, setting ablaze the hearts of our comrades, until the regular constitution of the assault battalions in 1917.

My first task when working on the preparation of my Arditi was that of moral education. This was facilitated by the selection of only the best elements in the army, who were gifted with that spirit for sacrifice which is at the core of every success in war. It was my personal endeavor to achieve such an education through regular contact with my troops and giving them an unflinching example. I believe I have succeeded in my task, with much help from my tireless officers and ensigns. For that, I thank you. Nothing was excluded from my drills. We practiced for every scenario we could think of; no possible danger we could have faced escaped my training.

Tactical instruction was extremely simplified. We went over elements previously learned, and what to apply during guerrilla operations. This is where ardimento and heart are most necessary, where perfect tactical forms are not enough. It was especially meant to practically demonstrate that fire sometimes pins down troops with negative results. It is better to resolutely push for the assault, reducing pauses to a bare minimum. The men suffer the most casualties, and the enemy has time to reorganize and take heart when troops are halted and cannot push forward.

This inflexible method was employed (to the point that I even took away cartridges from my soldiers) so that I could obtain incredible results. For example, in the action on Mount Collo, a position conquered after a fifteen-hour march in high snow and bitter cold against superior forces in reinforced positions, my losses were reduced to a couple wounded and dead. In the Glockenthurm action, I broke through two enemy lines in quick succession, pushing myself inside enemy positions many marching hours away from our own lines, sowing panic and destruction in the enemy's ranks and forcing him to waste a fantastic quantity of ammunition and artillery. During the two-day raid that I led on the slopes of Mount Collo, we pushed deep into enemy lines, even reaching the Austrian Superior Command posts. I returned in an orderly fashion, securing my company from counterattacks, and carrying away my dead and wounded. Finally, after three days of vicious fighting on Saint Osvaldo, I managed to push into the trenches of that important position. Defended by numerous troops and hit by a crown of artillery guns, it was ultimately conquered, but at the horrific and tragic cost of my company being destroyed.

The tactical objective assigned to my company, during its eight months of continuous combat, was to ensure the occupation of the positions dominating the Borgo Basin and, ultimately, conquering Saint Osvaldo to facilitate our ascent to Panarotta. To reach it, I had to attack and occupy all the mountainous regions that dominated the Borgo Basin: Montalon, Mount Collo, the Glockenthurm, Marter, Volto, and Mount Saint Osvaldo. The objective was reached. General Graziani stated that the company, with its conquest of Mount Collo, Volto and Mount Saint Osvaldo, "gave much respite to our troops in that sector and gave the division the possibility to engage in further operations."

I add to this that General Graziani also, in the months of May and June of 1916, held Mount Collo from being attacked in its extreme left flank by the Austrians, who aimed to take Mount Cima and flank our lines on the summit. Mount Collo, Volto, and Mount Saint Osvaldo were the three glorious conquests of the company, triumphantly crowning the cycle of operations tasked to it, even though the last of these was its tomb.

A New Factor for Victory

The order to institute the company in September 1915 enunciated the scope and the character of this department:

> Tasked with daring to succeed in ardite operations:
> reconnaissance, taking point in dangerous locations, ambushes,
> reinforcing troops in danger, etc....an autonomous company is
> instituted to which are destined elite soldiers from all armies and
> departments of the division, which have made voluntary request
> of transfer and possess the necessary requisites on judgment of
> Captain Baseggio...

From this order, we derive the tactical reasons and the educational
reasons. The company was not just an excellent instrument of war, but
most of all a true and practical school for arditismo.

It is also reiterated by the text of the speech I gave to the survivors
of Saint Osvaldo when I disbanded the company.

The Arditi let themselves be known as a new factor for victory. For
their willful actions they were united in regiments, and later in brigades
and divisions. They were recognized officially by that name that was
before only echoed along the cliffs of the Fassa Alps and in the Sugana
Valley: Arditi.

The black star that decorated the arm of my Arditi, was replaced by
a black flame. Even if the symbol had changed, the spirit of the Arditi,
who had their baptism in blood for two years, had not changed. They
finally had their official recognition and became elite squads among our
vast army.

Even after the end of the war, the mission of arditismo did not end.
In fact, the Arditi were the initiators of that redemption that, under my
leadership and the leadership of Benito Mussolini, Ferruccio Vecchi,
Mario Carli, and Marinetti, routed the subversive masses and
blossomed into the Fascist political movement. We must not forget the
sixty-five courageous men who came together on March 23th, 1919 for
the "Conference for the Constitution of the Fasces" held by Benito
Mussolini in Milan. To them we should add the two hundred Arditi who
guarded the streets and the plaza of San Sepolcro, ready to defend their
comrades locked in the hall to deliberate.

Finally, I can place my conscience at peace; a conscience that scolded
me for not having exalted the actions of my company for eleven years
and now inspires me to remember their sacrifices here.

I would like to repeat what then Lieutenant Orazio Pedrazzi wrote
in 1916, when he witnessed our actions:

The company returned to their trenches, carrying the dead bodies of their officers. It was then that the company was dissolved.

Each one of them returned to their regiment, carrying with them the tragic and fascinating memory of their beloved company.

No officer received a reward. Maybe there was no time to think about these things, or maybe too many were deserving of a medal.

The Arditi left just as they had arrived, as Garibaldi would have, giving up everything and getting nothing in return.

Near the kind village where they were billeted, in the flowery cemetery, there are some tombs lying next to one another. These hold the sacred bodies of those officers who fell in the Saint Osvaldo Assault. No one cuts the grass there anymore, after the exodus of the population. The overgrowth covers the little mounds of these heroes with greenery and flowers.

Upon the mountain, in those graves with no names, where the bodies of our men were thrown by the Austrians, lay dozens of volunteers who wanted to win; and to win, they had to die.

Those tombs, those graves, they are the medals of valor for the Death Company.

Oh Comrades, in giving you my heartfelt and loving goodbye, I urge you to raise a reverent thought for our Unforgettable Dead, who are with us in spirit and answer to my call. Remember Umerini, Galante, Galluzzo, Divina, Spader, Cugusi, and Vismara. Oh, remember all the fallen of the Death Company.

Appendix C:
Letter by Mario Dei Gaslini

Popolo d'Italia, May 25th, 1929
The Death Company

In every nation, there is a man born of their wars and epic struggles, who jumps from the fiercest of realities to reach otherworldly skies where he becomes a legend. The entirety of our war comes back to life in this atmosphere of heroic deeds and sublime figures. They all draw from the same Italian tradition, which gave us the saint, the apostle, the captain, the prince, the artisan, and the master artist in every era. All wars, in exemplifying the qualities of every man's ancestry, have confirmed greatness in many, and have sculpted figures that have excelled in every regard. They stand out in the backgrounds of paintings. They carve their way, from drawn silhouettes, out of the hard-pressed golden medals on which they are engraved. The Italian Ardito is certainly one of these figures. He is a knight of ideals: half poet, half soldier of fortune. He is a missionary, with a commanding will to fight, striving for victory amid battle. He does not give quarter. He does not surrender. He seeks neither reward nor accolades.

In war literature, of which there is an immense amount, with definitive significance at some points, the particularistic vision of the theatrical scene is missing. I say, if war justly represents the nation leaping to defend its borders, its rights, its treaties, its honor, and collective dignity, is it not also equally just that those collective groups (in the case of infantry, artillery, staff, aviation, etc.), maintain their pride, and some of their traditions, as well as the actions they took to fashion and maintain them?

Arditismo is an exclusively Italian phenomenon. Idealism led to its creation. For its war merits, which made it more and more a point of pride for us, it is an achievement that sparked hope in everyone's hearts in the darkest of hours. It has scant documentation in Italy, if we exclude the works and the pertinent chapters of those books with larger and more general aims. I remember only a little booklet by Mario Carli, a book by Cesare Solari, one by Ferruccio Vecchi, a volume by Paolo Giudici, and a few other publications. Now comes the one by Cristoforo Baseggio, entitled *The Death Company*.

When an author is judged, it is not rare to find between the different criticisms, either from an image or by the harshness of a phrase, the true profile of the man, his actions, his destiny, and his life. It is here that we find the man, right from the first page, in a citation by Petöfi, that might as well be the motto for our dangerous style of living: "The world is an ancient palace that overhangs from above. Walking straight ahead you will hit your head on its beam, so you will bend before the beam that is about to hit you. I would rather break my forehead than bend my back."

Cristoforo Baseggio was a soldier best described by the latter part of that quote. Indeed, it best describes both he and all his Arditi. He had firm arms, a ready mind, a heart made of pure heroism and a vibrant humanity. These are the qualities that made him a commander of heroes and now make him share his memories with the world. It is out of an earthly need to love again, to dare again, to document and to not let anyone forget again. In his magnificent preface, Giovanni Borelli sculpts the man beautifully. From the glow of that warrior's image, Borelli praises the elements of Baseggio's work simply as they stand. Here it is plain to see, alive and unmoved before the storm of battle, Cristoforo Baseggio: creator, and commander of the first "Death Company." This book provides one last ritual of love from him, and it crackles with an even greater passion as these memories are knit together to recount the greatness of the company's actions.

In the words of Borelli, Baseggio's "writing flows forth to fashion an altar to those who shed their blood and lost their lives fighting to take Saint Osvaldo." It has a style similar to the actions and the hearts of the heroes which make it up, which fill it to the brim, which render it as a banner, which make it as red as vermillion and consecrate it. Even his writing style, never rhetorical, just simple, almost manages to keep the taste and smell of the earth and flesh intact. It has a strange beauty all its own. Like bullets leaving a machine gun, the words sometime stutter and spit forth in a frenzy. At other times, they flow peacefully and tranquilly forth. To add to this, Borelli says:

The pages written by Baseggio imbibe themselves with a swelling and athletic *quid*, which determines the character and the intimacy of a bitter and disdainful style. That style sears its way through his account like a hot flame but then shines forth like a flash of thunder. It tastes of sun and glacier. It liberates from the magnanimous heart a sublime love for country and glory, with no equals in the world.

This book is unparalleled and is born from a legendary reality and from a real legend. It must not be fully exhausted. Baseggio says,

> The facts herein recorded have no greater value, in and of themselves, than many other facts of war and would not need to be highlighted, if it were not for the fact that they consecrate an idea. They are the expression of an act of faith and further proof that *arditismo, the exaltation of personal valor and the spirit of sacrifice,* opposed in war the stagnant tendencies that accompanied a military education and discipline more formal than substantial.

The volume, written "for a sense of duty towards the dead and for a sense of justice towards the survivors" has its own high raison d'être, and with its inherent quality, it finds its significance in the historical documentation of the war.

When Italy's destiny flew high into the skies of victory, the Arditi came many times to seize it out of the air, fashioning a *gagliardetto*[70] out of it, so that it could be planted on the achieved high peak.

After winning the war and the Revolution, our Arditi wanted to know if Italy still loved them as she did when she first blessed them?

Cristoforo Baseggio, your book may answer this question for the entire Italian nation.

Mario Dei Gaslini

---

[70] [A small rectangular or triangular flag used by battalions to show their emblems and motto.]

Appendix D:
Poem by G. Vacchetta to the Death Company

Heroes of the Sugana Valley

Mentre nel ciel fa smufar di rose
Quasi vapor di scintillanti gemme
Sale il sol fra le nebbie vaporose
E da lungi le cime biancheggianti
Indora, coi suoi raggi mattutini;
Mentre del primo augel su fra gli abeti
Riverdeggianti a primavera nuova
Si leva il canto che il mattin salute;
Per la pendice madida e impertlata
Dal pianto delle stele tremolanti
Sale la schiera sacra a nuovi fati
Silenziosa e canta alla conquista
Della vetta agognata che l'aspetta.
Bello è il mattino: un trionfar di sole
Che part di nuova luce irradiato
Dalla terra pel ciel sale un arcano
Fidente nel suo fato e nel suo duce,
Nuovo profumo di natura in fiore:
La bruna schiera sale arditamente,
Seguendo l'orma nel terren calcato
Da lui che Marcia al suo destin sicuro.
Tutto è silenzio. Par che un nuovo fato
Sia scritto innanzi a quegli eroi silent;
Ognun pronta ha la mano; o vita o morte.

Heroes of the Sugana Valley

The sun rises above a foggy mist
From which depart gems by sparkles kissed
I saw the rosy sky of the dearly missed
In faraway peaks where white snow hissed
Morning rays shining where souls reminisced
While above pines first fledgling lit
Sang a hail for the morning dawn
Blossoming all around new spring's first quip;
Along the pearly slope wet
With tears of shaking stones
Climbed holy ranks, faithful souls
Silently singing to conquer the threat
Of a coveted peak waiting for them.
Beautiful morning rises: sun is triumphant
With a new light he is donned
From earth to sky rises beyond
A spirit in fate and dux[71] confident
New smell of nature blossoming:
Brownish ranks climb arditely,
Of him who walks towards a sealed fate
Following steps on sunken soil
Men march, men toil
All is silence. A new faith seemingly
Written before those silent heroes,

---

[71] [Latin for "leader."]

Non parla il Duce, sol cammina innanzi
Dritto, come la lama della spade
Pronto ed alla percossa e alla parata.
E' San'Osvaldo là sulla pendice
Alto fra I faggi bruni e I Verdi abeti
Tristo come minaccia e come sfida;
A lui sale la schiera ardita e muta
A destin sacro, come un dì salia
Di Roma santa ai colli, la coorte,
Sempre invitta e gentil, di Garibaldi.
Sente nel core a sè sfuggir la vita
Ognun che sale—e quasi seduttrice,
Venere bell ache ogni gioia apporta
La morte ingannatrice che lo attira.
O bella morte, canta l'arma a tutti,
A me ti volgi—tanto sei bella,
Se da te vien la vita alla mia terra.
Croscia pel monte omai la mitragliera
E crepita il fucile, sibilando,
Invisibil per l'aria; messagero
Di morte il piombo infido passa.
Pare che arda ogni fusto, ogni roveto
E geme crepitando per l'ardore:
Romba il cannone lungi come tuono
E piove ferro sui salenti eroi.
Come a un mandorlo in fior, se
Mosso al vento, candide cadon le corolla
Al suolo, sì che poche ne resta
A recar frutto, tal della schiera tacita
Ed invitta cadono I vinti.
La mitraglia li spazza ad uno ad uno;
I prodi eran trecento,
Ogni passo che fanno uno ne cade.
Io tutti quanti vorrei cantare
Giovani eroi dall'incrollabil fede.
Voi che alla patria date e braccio e vita
E radioso venti primavera
Che april co' vaghi fiori suoi corona.

All with hands ready; life or death.
Their dux does not speak, he only walks
Upright, like a sword's blade
To strike and to parry ready.
It is Saint Osvaldo there on the peak
High among dark beeches and green pines
Bleak how it menaces and challenges
To him climb the ranks ardite and mute
To sacred destiny, as days past
The cohorts did rise, to saintly Rome's hills,
Always undefeated and kind, of Garibaldi.
Feel in one's heart life escaping
As one climbs—almost seductive,
Beautiful Venus gives joy to all
Yet it is death deceivingly calling him near
Oh, sweet death, sing of life to all
How pretty as you turn to me,
From death comes my country's life.
Stutters down the mountain as always, the gun
And rifles crack, whistling
Invisible messenger: travels the air
Of death the insidious lead passes.
Every trunk looks ablaze, every bush
Moans crackling for the ardor
Like an almond tree blooming, when
Moved by the wind, candidly fall crowns
On ground, for little are left
To bear fruit, same as that silent
Undefeated rank, fall the vanquished
The machine gun sweeps them one by one,
There were three hundred brave
At every step one fell.
Of all I would like to sing
Young heroes of unshakeable faith
You who have given aid and life
And those radiant twenty springs
That April with mixed flowers crowns
Do not cry for your dead, oh mothers

Non li piangete o madri, I vostri morti
Questi che morte alla vittoria sacra
Nascendo I cor colle viole
Sono I martiri nostril, I nostril santi,
Dei del nostro Olimpo puro e grande.
Dal sangue lor germoglieran le rose
A coronar l'Italia ancor più forte;
Chi per la Patria muor vive in eterno.
Vorrei cantarvi tutti con gran voce
O ignoti eroi, che il sacrificio col dover giungete.
Galante cui consudde aspro destino
Di tua vita nel baratro
Col petto aperto mentre gridi "Avanti!"
Ai tuoi clamanti eroi sulla trincea.
E Gagliotti ferito dall'insidia
Del teutone assassin, che combatti
Finchè nel sangue tuo non cadi esangue?
O Gloria, a me accorri! O mente aiuta
la mia penna che canta I pochi eletti!
Di Umerini il passo e la caduta
Rotta la fronte di pensier sì forte,
E canto di Galluzzo, ultimo eletto
Che il masso rotolante uccise invitto
Presso toccar la vetta desiata
Del miglior del tuo sangue consacrata.
E Signorelli che ferito ancora
Cure I feriti e non pon mente a sè,
E Rabajoli imberbe che piangemmo
Un istante perduto, e che d'un balzo
Con Quattro uomini suoi coi suoi feriti,
Carco dell'arme dei nemici uccisi
Torna ridente.
Sì, vorrei cantar miei dolci amici
Come cantava il dì che conobbi
A gran voce, il cannone,
E il nome Vostro confidare all'eco
Che lo ripeterebbe per le valli
Giungendo fino alle ansiose madri

These whom death desired for victory sacred
Their hearts born as violets are
They are our martyrs, our saints,
Gods of our pure and grand Olympus.
From their blood will blossom roses
To crown an even stronger Italy;
Whomsoever dies for country lives forever.
I want to sing you all with mighty voice
Oh, unknown heroes, that sacrifice with duty united
Galante lead to cruel destiny
His life down an abyss
With open chest you shouted "Forward!"
To your aching soldiers in trenches
Gagliotti was wounded by treachery
By the Teuton killer, what to fight for
If you do not fall bleeding on your own blood?
Oh glory, come to me! Oh, mind help
My pen in writing of the chosen few!
Of Umerini his step and fall
Cracked his head his thoughts were so strong,
I sing of Galluzzo the last chosen
That rolling boulder killed undefeated
Close to touching the so desired peak,
By the rest of our blood consecrated.
Signorelli wounded and yet
Healed the wounded with no care of himself
Rabajoli the hairless for whom we cried,
In one moment lost, but with a flash
With four men and his wounded
Full of defeated enemy's weapons
Came back laughing.
Yes, I would like to sing of my dear friends
Like I sang the day I met them
With great voice, the cannon
Your names I would give to echo
He would repeat them along the valleys
Reaching those anxious mothers
With their ears peaked waiting

Che tendon l'orecchio ad aspettare,
E lor direi: siate superbe, o donne,
Dale viscere vostre uscì l'eroe
Che nel nome d'Italia vines e cadde
Su l'aspro monte ove la neve ancora
Manteneva il candor.
Presso gli abeti, ci mancava un colore
Alla bandiera
Il Vostro sangue e goccie di rubini ce l'ha portato
Consacrando le zolle benedette
A l'Italia più grande e più possente.

G. Vacchetta
Of the Explorers Company Arditi Baseggio
Borgo, the Sugana Valley (April 1916)

To them I would say: be proud, women,
From your insides came the hero
Who for Italy's sake fell and won
On that cruel mount where snow
Still kept his warmth
Among the pines, one color missed
From the flag
Your blood like drops of rubies
Brought it
Consecrating the holy land
Of Italy greater and mightier.

G. Vacchetta
Of the Explorers Company Arditi Baseggio
Borgo, the Sugana Valley (April 1916)